Naked articles on our financial times: 2008-2013.

John G Smith

Disclaimer

All persons and organisations mentioned in this
book are real. If I have caused offence to any
party, this was unintentional and not wilful.

All events described in this work reflect my
honest recollection and interpretation.

ISBN: 978-1-291-61451-0

This book is dedicated to Oliver James

- of the smart new generation who will be astounded at our stupidity.

I wish to thank once again David Robinson for his technical skill and sound advice throughout the creation of this book.

Copyright, reproduction and sale conditions.

Egmanton   November 2013

Author's note.

As the often crazy world of finance and economics unfolded in the five-year period 2008-2013, I waited to be hit (often stunned) by a piece of breaking news or by some particular event. This in turn would trigger a response (sometimes a very mental one) from me in the form of an article placed on my website www.quantitative-wheezing.co.uk.

This little book pulls these articles together. Because each one was written at a point in time, what has actually happened since is itself testament to the changing times.

Contents.

Part 1

Prelude for the thrusting executive
The corporate survival kit.

Never, ever, play internal politics.
The higher one climbs up the corporate ladder, so the likelihood increases of being drawn into a cadre that will be in competition with or even in conflict with some other group of executives. Indeed, if functional reporting relationships are in play, it is a virtual certainty that you will forced to go with one side and against another. Whilst this can be healthy and invigorating, it can also be highly dangerous.

This danger lies not in having to make a stand or having to support one view against another but rather in making personal indirect attacks by setting off rumours or by other forms of innuendo. It might seem clever at the time and it might pay off for quite a while but at some stage in the future and most probably when you least expect it, there will be a knife between your shoulder-blades

See www.quantitative-wheezing.co.uk for ten more tips on corporate survival.

The House Built on Sand.

Let's think about the New Testament parable (Matthew 7.24-27).

"The wise man built his house on stone. Then a great flood came there, and winds blew there, and fell down upon the house, and it did not fall: truly, it was built on stone.

Then the foolish man built his house on sand Then it rained, and a flood came there, and winds blew, and fell down upon the house, and the house fell; and its fall was great".

And there were these great big UK builders of houses, Persimmon, Taylor Wimpey, Barratt, Bellway, Bovis and Redrow and they enjoyed many, many good years. Demand for homes exceeded supply due largely to archaic planning laws, too few planning officers and for those that did exist too little commercial nouse and with fire-in-belly long since doused and so, where development took place, ticky-tacky houses grew like the slums of old and massed together with no room to breath, no room to grow and no room to swing a cat.

People who knew the industry would say that out of the selling price to these new slum dwellers, one third went on the cost of the land, one third on building the tat and the final third was clear profit. Of-course that may be an exaggeration but certainly net profit margins were exceedingly high and the good times did roll.

So why was it that when the rains came, the great builders fell like the proverbial pack of cards? It is because our dear and much lamented friend Prudence went walkies, she sauntered into the flood and was never seen again and how those that sent her into the storm must regret their lack of caution.

You see, all that lovely lolly went walkies along with our Prudence. It went in the direction of directors' fees, management salaries, generous dividends to the loyal shareholders (not forgetting the share options) and finally and most fatally it went on our old and faithfully intangible friend Goodwill. see *"How to read a Balance Sheet* on Quantitative-Wheezing.co.uk".

What goodwill? Well, the elusive difference in price between what the net assets are worth and what we have decided to pay for our competitor so that we can gobble him up and make ourselves even bigger and stronger, better able to pay out more bunce. Get it?

For example there was once a builder called Westbury. A very successful provincial builder with ideas above its station, it even had buildings put up off-site and built in a factory to reduce the inefficiency of labour intensive activity on site. By dint of its very own success, it was expensive to gobble up; but it was so gobbled and the goodwill was immense. It took much of the profit reserves of Big Builder to acquire.

But this was only one of many acquisitions by Big Builder or, put in more sanguine tones, only a small part of reasonable "rationalisation" of the industry. Yet there is no natural logic to bigness if it takes away the profit of the past in a trade whose cyclical nature is as old as the proverb itself. Why was the fat of the good times not put aside for the lean years that had to come? Why was the house built on sand?

About Brazil.

We all know that there is an awful lot of coffee in Brazil. What is less well known is that there are, increasingly, an awful lot of other things as well.

The chattering classes within the investment circles are increasing voicing the acronym BRIC's. Three letters stand for the rapidly emerging markets of China, India and Russia, how did the dark horse of Brazil enter the frame?

Most importantly we must think about oil supplies. Whilst it is reported widely that output from the non-OPEC trio of Norway, Britain and Mexico has fallen relentlessly over the past few years, a group of other countries is gradually breaching the shortfall. And which country heads the list of increases in oil production measured in millions of barrels per day? The answer is Brazil.

For the switched on investor with a global interest, an investment trust rather than picking individual companies seems to be the ideal answer. For example, the Black Rock Latin American fund has increased in value over the past five years by 650%.

The point about this "Latin America" fund is that it is dominated by Brazil. In fact 8 of the top 10 holdings are wholly or mainly Brazilian focused. The sectors covered are:-

* Mining

* Wireless communication

* Energy (oil and others)

* Private sector banking

* Steel production

* Beverages

* Railway operation

　　So next time you have a coffee, think about that next long-haul holiday you have so deservedly earned. Yes it could be China or India or Russia (at a push). For me, I am off to Brazil to check on my investments. When did you say the Rio festival was?

What Is Commercial Fraud?

Where is a line drawn between sloppy accounting or (say) misguided optimism or simple naivety and a downright intention to mislead, or put another way, the deliberate act of committing commercial fraud?

According to Simon Bevan of leading accountants BDO and as reported in the Daily Telegraph on 4th August 2008, the financial extent of commercial fraud far outstrips the effect of mortgage fraud, ATM fraud and credit card fraud. Commercial fraud is estimated to cost Britain's banks £2bn a year.

The "white collar" fraudsters hit a bank's corporate lending department by inflating asset valuations (i.e. a Balance Sheet action) and overstating income predictions (i.e. a Profit & Loss and Budget and Forecast action). Furthermore, Mr Bevan says that lenders rarely recover the losses since they need to be chased through the civil courts.

A fraudulent act may start as a simple deception to get as much debt as possible. It seems that banks are reluctant to confront commercial fraud head on as it is often conducted in concert with employees and exposes poor lending standards "Banks' credit committees often don't want to admit they have been defrauded". Last week both Lloyds TSB and HBOS reported a doubling in bad debts in their corporate lending divisions. It is claimed that cheats operate in collusion with solicitors and accountants who may have provided "dodgy" business plans, and valuers who overvalue assets alongside internal staff who are willing to turn a blind eye to claims that are obviously false.

In the period 1992 to 2002 I prepared many business plans for small to medium sized enterprises and initially under the auspices of a subsidised scheme run by the then DTI. A sound business plan pulls all the aspirations for the future into one document and crucially concludes with the numbers. It is at that point that all the challenging of assumptions should take place.

Cavalry charge from the East.

That mainland Europe is drowning in debt is not news. That the peripheral countries of Europe have had to, and are expected to continue to, kowtow to the central bank and the IMF for survival finance is also not news. What is news is that poor old Portugal (apparently the UK's oldest ally) eschewed this assumed creditor route and announced a private placement of 1.1bn euros of debt issued in the form of bonds. In one sense it was an act of sheer bravado not least because the big boys of Germany and France are vetoing a larger pool of money for the rescue plan of the Southern Mediterranean countries.

In the event, the placement is thought to have been oversubscribed by a factor of two. And here is the key component. According to the Wall Street Journal, the secret buyer of the Portuguese debt was China. Why? There are a number of theories and some are political to do with the current arms embargo but what is certain is that China has openly pledged to use part of its £1.82 trillion of reserves to safeguard global stability.

Portugal is not alone in being on the receiving end of an Eastern cavalry charge to assuage the financial meek of, in particular, Germany. Madrid has just sold 3bn euros of debt and Italy too found it surprisingly easy to finance its deficit.

Who knows what the real intention of the middle kingdom is but added to its cornering of the world market in rare metals and its increasing ownership of world supply commodities, there has to be an outlet for its vast reserves or else its currency will balloon out of control and damage its vital export trade. Why not support sickly Europe? And, by the way, the EU has just lifted its high tariff on Chinese shoes. The next move on the Chinese chess table might concern India and toys!

The $700bn USA bank bail-out.

No matter what all the experts had to say in favour of the Paulson bale-out plan, how does smallish individual piles of rubbish improve by being placed together in one big pile? If there might be profit to be made from the big pile eventually, then the same would happen to a small pile – wouldn't it?

The big argument in favour is if the rubbish is taken from the banking world then that world will suddenly free itself up. I do not think so, there is too much fear and mistrust about.

The taxpayer versus the shareholder will continue to rage but in the end shareholders are taxpayers and when the common man goes bust, there is only the State left to pick up his financial burden. But it does seem better to have the taxpayer pick up the bill gradually over time than in one big lump, i.e. pile of rubbish.

Stock Market Angst.

James Bartholomew writes an occasional article in the Saturday issue of the Daily Telegraph under the heading "Diary of a Private Investor". On October 25th 2008 he wrote "It is frightening to see large chunks of one's wealth disappear overnight. I have lost, regained and re-lost sums of money that are, to me, very substantial". Overall, it is a very angry article. Angry with himself, angry with the Government and, as it happens, angry with BBC presenters. The tenet is that people who have lost a lot of money often need to sell anything to raise cash to survive and so perpetuate the already dire position of perfectly good shares.

In the summer of this year I was writing about holding a portfolio of "value" shares for their yield and awaiting the good times to roll again. The only manner in which I am not quite as angry as James is attributable to a conscious decision to liquidate those share that had performed well (done in September 2007) and store the cash. But I am angry too since the shares of really good companies that I retained have been hit for no good sound economic reasons. I am slightly placated by not needing to sell any of them, and I do not intend to.

But the damage is palpable (as it must be with my personal pension fund that I refuse to look at). Overall my portfolio is down 58% with the largest casualties being Taylor Wimpey -89%, Sterling Energy -86% and Yell Group -57%. No wait, my holding in Black Rock Latin American Investment Trust is down 62% and before all this lot started it was up 20%.

The point about this article is that James and I are not alone. If such reasonably sophisticated investors as we can be so wrong, what about the less informed folk out there?

The ludicrous practice of the share buy-back.

The fashion for a company to buy-back its own shares is, in my view, financial stupidity in the extreme. You could say that this judgement comes with the benefit of hindsight, but actually not so. I have an interest in a Leisure Sector business that recently bought back a substantial tranche of its own shares. To do so, it borrowed a huge sum of money and of course cancelled the shares in question. It seemed to me stupid at the time and is catastrophically stupid now.

Aside from the cynical point that most parties benefited financially from the buy-back transaction, that is to say, city advisers, management as incentivised on earnings-per-share performance and institutional investors for a brief time, any logical oversight would conclude that the transaction was artificial. If the shares at the time were worthy of purchase, why was not Joe ordinary investor buying? Exactly one year ago, 77 companies were purchasing their own shares. The FTSE stood at 6,300. To give just two examples (there are plenty more), Alliance & Leicester were buying at 614p (one year earlier they bought their own shares at more than £12). A&L was sold to Santander at 317p and HBOS was buying its shares at 783p and these shares have since dropped by about 90%.

Debt from trading or service providing is one thing, debt from financial engineering is quite another.

Prime the fiscal pump whilst the debt tank is full of water!

I have to hold my hand up. Whatever brickbats I have to suffer in the future for this misjudgement, I do not agree with the fiscal stimuli that are going to be announced for the UK in a pre-budget statement next Monday. That is, unless it is specifically and solely directed to the housing market; which it will not be. It matters not whether the quantum is £1, £1bn or the mooted £100bn. It matters not if there is a plan to recoup it. Having pumped huge loans into the lenders, the market should now take care of itself. The market must decide where things go from here, it always has and it always will. To throw money in terms of tax give-a-ways to a particular group of people in the certain belief that they will spend it, is madness. Actually it represents the root cause of the present disease, that is spend and borrow, spend and borrow, and sod tomorrow

Consider this tank of debt. In 1990/91, Government debt was 26% of GDP. By 2007/08, this level had reached 43% of GDP. But, this level does not include the "off-balance sheet" Government borrowing which, according to the Centre for Policy Studies, and after adding the latest round of loans to and investments in banks, means that actually government debt is 127% of GDP. Now add to this the personal debt of the UK average Joe. Ten years ago it was 60% of GDP; now it is 100%. Thirdly, the banks themselves are much more highly borrowed than even two years ago.

And we intend to encourage people to follow the profligate practice of the Government and the big lenders in the expectation they will start buying houses and cars again. Mindblowingly stupid in my opinion and very, very dangerous.

National Air Traffic Services (NATS) – the position of an ordinary shareholder.

There has been some commentary between members of the Employee Share Trust about the valuation of their individual holding and whether it seems sensible to sell out. As a complete outsider with no detailed knowledge of the financial strength of the business, it is not possible to offer advice. Yet, the observations of the ignorant might be helpful since standing aloof and being objective may have a place.

First, NATS is a Public Private Partnership (PPP). This means it falls into the category of part Government owned, part private. This Government has launched many of these schemes and not least in the structure domain, such as hospitals and schools. The central role in such financing can be criticised due to the taxpayers' element being placed "off balance sheet" which means that the liability of the investment is not shown as part of Government indebtedness. On the other hand, neither is the asset value. Some PPPs have been sold on at a profit but mainly by the private party.

What does all this matter to the shareholder? Well, in the case of NATS, the Government owns 49%. To all intents this means that the business is nationalised (as for example so is the Royal Bank of Scotland after the public bail-out). Furthermore, 42% is held in a block vote called The Airline Group and 4% by BAA. This leaves the ordinary employee shareholder with a very minor holding of 5%. A holding with no influence in a business with no free market for the shares. Shareholder value is therefore in the hands of others.

It is not possible to value an individual share from the limited information available in the public domain, for example the number of share in issue is not stated on the website, although a search of the statutory listing would reveal this information. But essentially the value will be meaningless until such time as a free market is established. This can only happen if and when the Government sells its stake, or a big slug of it, and The Airline Group agree to do likewise. The BAA holding is irrelevant.

There has been some speculation about a whole valuation. Again, one has to assume a free market for the shares. In the most recent year 07/08 the group profit is shown as £66.7m and if we assume an effective tax charge of (say) 20% and a PE of 15 (both these assumptions are challengeable), a figure of £801m arises. However, the profit in that year was much less than in 06/07 which was reported as £94.4m and it could be that there were exceptional items in the later year. If the 06/07 year is taken as a basis and the same assumptions on tax and price earnings used, the valuation would be £1.13bn.

But that is not what a buyer would pay for at least two reasons. First, there is a stated net debt of £538.1m at the end of the 07/08 year and an investment programme costing £1bn spread over ten years. A buyer would look carefully at both the future cost of servicing the debt and absolute cashflow.

Finally, on the timing of any sale of their shares, an employee should consider that merger and acquisition activity is at a low ebb and not likely to pick up until late 2009. All the portents therefore scream out HOLD ON.

India is booming Mr Smith.

So said the Indian gentleman go-between for the large Indian group that succeeded in buying a business located in London that I was brokering the sale of.

The Indian continent was not foreign to me, or rather a bit of it wasn't. If you turn to page 229 of my book Barn Door To Balance Sheet, the adventure in Cochin in the Southern State of Kerala begins. So I was very pleasantly surprised to have to work with the Indian gentleman and to have an inkling on how to apply a little pressure in the Indian style. I mention this since the partially true statement that India was "booming Mr Smith, booming" has had at least one surprising consequence.

It is reported that the disgraced former chairman of Indian IT company Satyam had a lavish collection of more than 1,000 designer suits. He also had 321 pairs of shoes, 310 belts and 13 cars including Mercedes and BMW's. His house contained a telescope worth £140,000 and a fully equipped gym. He had donated huge quantities of gold to temples in Andhra Pradesh and built up a property portfolio including palatial mansions and villas spanning 63 countries. The profits of Satyam had been overstated for years and $1bn of cash and bank balances did not exist. Mr Ramalinga Raju admitted falsifying the accounts of the company he founded. He stands accused of siphoning off $4m each month in the names of 13,000 non-existent workers.

Booming Mr Smith, booming.

The great "rights issue" ding dong.

There is a long-standing tradition with the stock market known as "pre-emption rights". Pre-emption rights allow existing shareholders to participate on equal terms in new fundraisings.

In recent times this tradition has not been observed in certain high profile cases. The most publicised has been the raising of funds from certain Middle Eastern sources by Barclays Bank disallowing any existing shareholder to participate. Not only that but the new funders were issued with tax-deductible securities which paid a coupon of 14%. So unfair was this seen to be that the City of London's largest institutional investor, Legal & General Investment Management, is understood to be calling for the resignation of the chairman of Barclays.

The accepted way to give all existing shareholders an opportunity to subscribe for new shares is known as a "rights issue". It is fair since these shareholders have risked their capital with the company in the past and furthermore the new shares or "rights" are invariably priced at a discount to the current market price. Arithmetically, if more shares are issued and the market capitalisation of a company stays the same, the share price of each share in issue must fall (total value divided by more shares). In such circumstances the existing shareholder can average down his holding by subscribing for the new rights. A reward for more finance in a company with an improved balance sheet.

A further ding dong of Barclays proportion is raging. It concerns Rio Tinto announcing an agreed deal with Chinalco, the state-controlled Chinese aluminium producer, such that Chinalco will inject $19.5bn by taking convertible bonds and a minority equity stake in nine mines. Major existing shareholders are furious and want the deal overturned in favour of a $10bn rights issue that they will support. What makes matters worse is that Rio Tinto rejected an offer by BHP of Australia the world's biggest miner. Existing shareholders believe a rights issue that strengthens the balance sheet will entice BHP back to the table. China of course has been taking stakes in mining companies around the world, not least in Africa, for the past 20-30 years to safeguard supply lines to their manufacturing base.

In this time of heavily indebted balance sheets, rights issues are, notwithstanding Barclays and Rio Tinto, in favour. Here is a list of companies that have issued rights in recent times :-

Xstrata, Workspace, Hammerson, British Land, Beazley, Catlin and Cookson and a list of those that are rumoured to be planning to issue rights:-

Liberty International, William Hill, Premier Foods, Land Securities, Legal and General and Segro.

For individual shareholders the offer of even heavily discounted rights presents a dilemma. Throw good money after bad or see your existing share price fall as the rest get cheap shares. It is not theoretical either. At this time I have to decide whether or not to take up the British Land rights that carry a discount of 53%.

Goodwill.

We are not talking about magnanimity but the accounting definition. Goodwill is the difference between what a business pays for another business and the deemed valuation of the assets in that business. For example, say we agree to buy XY Co Ltd for £5m and the value we place on the fixed assets (land and buildings, plant and machinery, fixtures and fittings, office equipment) and the net current assets (cash, stock and debtors less liabilities) comes to £4.5m. The accounting entries would be credit cash, or some other funding method, and debit the asset categories. But what about the gap of £0.5m? Plonk it in Goodwill .

Goodwill is what it says on the tin. Accountants call it an "intangible" asset. Definition number 2 in the Collins Dictionary is "capable of being clearly grasped by the mind". That is precisely right in the converse. If you cannot quite grasp why you paid that extra £0.5m, pretend it really was worth it and create an asset called Goodwill. Joe ordinary bloke will be hoodwinked. It will look really good all presented nice and clean and standing proud at the head of the real assets.

Once we have created our Goodwill, what to do with it? This is beautiful, you will like this one. Let's write it off in equal instalments over twenty years. That way old Joe will just think our blue sky was just another bit of the regular depreciation or, if we want to be posh, amortisation. Now, if Goodwill created on a purchase is just a few pence, who cares?

Yesterday the Treasury Select Committee of UK MP's grilled the former bosses of RBS on the purchase of ABN Amro. Did they overpay? The ex-Chairman of RBS replied "Whatever we paid, we overpaid". In hindsight, whatever the figure of Goodwill struck at the time, think of a number. Think of a big number. What about £5bn to £7.5bn? In fact, when the accounts came out, the write-off of Goodwill was £16bn. Now that is what I call intangible.

The positive investor.

One of the earliest pieces published on my website www.Quantitative-Wheezing.co.uk was called "UK Stockmarket History". The idea was to give readers who were not familiar with investing and financial terminology generally, a basis for understanding what they were likely to be reading about and hearing about as the credit crunch crisis unfolded. Within that background reading was a heading "Choosing an investment strategy" and two such strategies covered were "Value investing" and "Contrarian investing". These two approaches to choosing which shares to buy have one thing in common: rowing against the tide and finding value for money.

Alan Steel, the founder of Alan Steel Asset Management, an independent financial adviser firm, wrote a piece in the Daily Telegraph cautioning investors to beware the prophets of doom on the basis that the numbers do not stack up. His main points were these:-

* Estimates both in UK and US suggest that stockmarkets are 42% too cheap.

* Corporate insiders are net buyers of shares in their own company.

* In 1930, the year of the great depression, US GDP fell by 9%, the next year it fell by 6.5%

and in 1932 it fell 13%. By contrast, in 2007 the US GDP rose 2% and last year it rose 1.5%.

* Currently, monetary policy is very loose with interest rates at almost zero.

* Job losses and mortgage foreclosures are far less than during the Great Depression.

* Unemployment in the US shows job losses of 600,000, the worst since 1974 but the US labour force is 65% greater now than in December of that year.

* Advertising is in decline and yet online advertising revenue is booming (the UK business Rightmove has just announced super figures, it is an online housing advertising site). In January 09, experienced investors in the US had 42% on deposit and on the last two occasions when they were at this level namely 1991 and 2002, it preceded the best two years to buy equities since 1987.

* The average gain in the stock market following an incoming Democrat president replacing an outgoing Republican is 13%, 126 days later.

Of course, any independent financial adviser has a vested interest in persuading you to have a punt, but still, even trying to think positively is a reason to be cheerful not least when the FTSE has dipped to below 4,000 and is less dominated by financials.

Warren Buffett agrees.

One of my previous articles was called "The ludicrous practice of the share buy-back". Now, in early May 09, the Sage of Omaha has said more or less the same. Speaking at the AGM of his investment vehicle Berkshire Hathaway, Mr Buffett said "Most of the repurchasing in recent years was foolish".

In the article of November last, I gave two examples of money-wasting buy-back decisions namely the building society Alliance & Leicester and the bank HBOS. Now on the back of this story from Omaha, the Daily Telegraph has come up with further examples. RBS launched a £1bn share buy-back in 2006 paying an average of £18.38 for the shares. These shares are now 44p. In January 2008, Lehman Brothers bought back 19% of its equity, nine months before it went bust.

The UK Shareholders' Association (UKSA) is on record as believing that the dividend route is the preferred way of returning cash to shareholders. As was stated back in November, buy-backs are criticised as a way to improve management benefits under share option or other remuneration schemes attached to earnings per share (less shares equal more earnings each).

Capitalising on the 50% tax band.

From April 2010 UK income tax will be 50% for high earners, defined as having earnings above £150,000 per year.

While there is no easy way to avoid this crippling rate short of leaving the country, which some are already planning to do and with Switzerland a favourite choice, thoughts must turn to the classic difference between "revenue" and "capital".

In the e-book "Debunking the balance sheet", the difference between revenue and capital was explained in relation to expenditure. Now we need to look at these definitions in relation to income and specifically "earned income" as opposed to income from sales.

A cornerstone feature of the UK tax system has always been the distinction of income from wages and profits from capital assets (those assets defined as capital expenditure when incurred). An investment in the equity shares of a company is a "capital" one. Such an investment has two spin-offs. First a dividend or share of profit of the company and secondly the appreciation in the market value of the share.

For some time now, share dividends have been regarded for tax purposes as a reward for risk taking and taxed at a lower rate than wages and salaries. The gain from a capital asset has been subjected to varying rates of tax over the years but is currently quite low. Where is all this leading?

High earners could take some of their pay as shares in the company they work for. Any capital gain will be taxed currently at 18% or 28% (higher rate payers) and the dividends will be taxed at an effective rate of 25% or next year at 32%.

Owners of a company could choose to pay themselves via dividends in part substitution for salary although it is more complicated than that since dividends are not tax deductible before the "taxable profit" is struck and corporation tax is payable on such profits.

Two other possibilities for capitalising on the top tax imposition is for the self-employed to incorporate themselves and pay corporation tax on profits (between 21% and 28% currently) and for partnerships to appoint a "corporate partner" for investment back into the firm (28% tax).

National Insurance levy and pension contributions must also be taken into account.

Employer's Covenant Review.

The Pensions Act 2004 places a requirement on trustees to assess the strength of the employer's covenant at the time of the actuarial valuation and indeed at any time when they might be concerned that the employer is no longer a going concern. The Pension Regulator's guidance to trustees of a scheme having a deficit is that they should negotiate with the employer in much the same way as would a bank having a large unsecured debt. The report to be requested is called an Employer Covenant Review (ECR).

The principal ingredient of the ECR is a forecast profit & loss account, cashflow and balance sheet. The latter is of the most use to check on how the other forecasts gel together. For example, how does the cash aspect of debtor and creditor movements in the balance sheet compare with the forecast turnover, cost of sales and operating costs? The second most vital forecast is the anticipated cashflow. Starting with the reconciled bank balance, examine critically all the forecasts of days in debtor recovery and days in creditor payments to test the feasibility of achievement. Especial emphasis must go on the "capital" elements of the expected forward cash such as interest rate changes, debt repayment deadlines or roll-overs and not least capital payments and commitments. It is vital to reconcile forecast profits with forecast cashflow.

No figures are better than the underlying assumptions on which they are based. Test these for realism rigorously. This means a shortish timeframe, usually only 1-2 years when compared to the maturity profile of a pension scheme. Where danger signals appear, liquidity outcomes are of the essence as is the pecking order of lenders to the company. An independent Business Review commissioned by a bank will always have payout priorities as a fulcrum. So also must the ECR.

A link between recession and fraud.

The big accountancy firm KPMG counts cases of serious fraud that come to court.

In the first half of 2009 there were 160 such cases, the highest number for 21 years. The volume is attributed to people increasingly desperate due to the economic recession.

Two cases were highlighted. A social worker invented a children's home to siphon off over £600,000 of public funds and a secretary who claimed to have cancer to get leave from work paid £600,000 into her own account by paying wages there. She paid for plastic surgery which one would not think of as a recessionary necessity.

Funny old world but makes an interesting change from bean-counting. '

Alleged Chinese corruption.

One of the UK's largest engineering companies has the innocuous name of Smiths Group. It is not an under-the-arches set-up. It has a market capitalisation of £2.8bn and sales of £2.3bn. One of its divisions makes x-ray scanners used at airports, ports and similar places where security is vital. Smiths have called foul on a Chinese company linked to the eldest son of the Chinese president Hu Jintao. This action has triggered an investigation by the EU into illegal dumping of such scanning equipment to the disadvantage of Smiths Group's own products. It is alleged that sales are made at a price advantage by offering a soft loan to the potential customer.

The Chinese company is called NucTech and is owned by the Chinese government. NucTech signed a contract with HM Revenue & Customs in 2006 to supply its machines to British ports and it has also held talks with BAA. The European investigation coincides with one of alleged corruption in Namibia. NucTech has also be probed in the Philippines after winning an airport security contract before it had been put to public tender.

Mergers & Acquisitions – Profit or Loss.

Common sense dictates that one is in the M&A business to generate synergies, cut costs, increase efficiency, benefit from economy of scale.

There used to be two independent UK companies that were leading brands and profitable. Very profitable. The AA and Saga need no introduction.

Along comes a company with a name you have never heard of "Acromas". It bought both the AA and Saga. It has just published its accounts for the year to January 09. Acromas made a pre-tax loss of £506m. This was caused not by trading in road-side assistance or holidays for the over 50's or financial services. It was caused by an interest bill just north of £700m.

Acromas has debts of more than £6bn. Common sense indeed.

Mortgage fraud.

According to accountants BDO, mortgage fraud will cost the UK a minimum of £1bn.

Buy-to-let has been the most fertile ground. Bradford and Bingley, the now nationalised lender, has written off £271m and the bulk of Chelsea Building Society's £53m of declared bad debts (half year to 30th June 09) was in its buy-to-let book.

How does such a fraud work? According to a piece by Philip Aldrick of the Daily Telegraph, a scheme could be as follows.

One landlord would, for example, put up £150,000 to buy a group of flats for £1m under a typical 85% mortgage offer. Keeping the properties in a "group", he sells them on for £1.2m.

The group is a collection of landlords brought together by an intermediary with the collusion of lawyers and valuers.

The flats are then sold on again for £1.5m before a final deal at £2m.

Each sale transaction is accompanied by a false valuation.

The mortgage lender (say Bradford & Bingley or Chelsea) puts up 85% of the final price or for these examples £1.7m which is of course £700,000 more than the initial valuation.

The flats are ultimately sold within the group for £2m and the consortium has never invested more than the initial £150,000.

The profit after tax of about £400,000 is split between buyers, sellers, valuers and lawyers and the intermediary.

The actual fraud will be large scale.

Fraudsters move their profit off-shore and declare bankruptcy.

The lender is left with properties with genuine valuations as little as half the mortgage value.

Something must have been a bit lax somewhere, methinks.

The demise of the final salary pension scheme.

The number of pension schemes based upon the level of final salary, that is, salary at retirement age or averaged over the last few years of earning life, continues to decline or be devalued. Such "defined benefit" schemes, using the jargon, now cover only three of the UK FTSE 100 companies for new members according to actuaries Lane Clark & Peacock. They are Tesco, Diageo and Cadbury. The three businesses that treat and indulge the body.

Another big firm of actuaries, Watson Wyatt, have forecast that half of all final salary schemes will be closed to existing members by 2012.

RBS, the 70% nationalised bank, have announced a downward move on their pension scheme that has been closed to new members since 2006. Affecting 62,500 staff, the rate of growth in pensionable salary will be capped at 2% a year or the annual rate of inflation, whichever is lower. This means regardless of pay rises. The move is costed to save RBS £100m a year. Alternatively, the staff can move to a defined contribution scheme and into which the employer will pay a generous 15% of salary. Actuaries think the change will produce a £500m one-off gain to boost the annual profit.

Staying with banks, Barclays is moving 17,000 staff into a hybrid scheme that should save the bank about £150m a year. A strike is threatened over this one.

One bit of good news is that the disgraced Sir Fred Goodwin agreed to forgo £4.7m of his top-up whilst still taking a £2.7m lump sum from RBS and an annual pension of £342,000.

The great pensions divide.

Over the past few years no subject has carried more column inches in the financial/social commentaries than the great and increasing pension divide.

Leading actuarial firms such as Hewitts, Watsons and Mercers have stressed the degree of the UK pensions apartheid.

Now the UK's leading accounting firm, and probably the global leader too, PricewaterhouseCoopers has published a new report on the subject. According to this report, private sector workers in "defined contribution" schemes receive, typically, employer contributions of 6% of salary. For civil servants contributing just 1.5% of salary to their "final salary" pension scheme, the implied employer contribution (that is to say the taxpayer) could be as high as 35.5%.

PwC compared the financial fortunes of a public sector employee who remains in civil service employment from age 21 to retirement at age 60 with someone born in the same year but who spends the whole working life in the private sector. The result is astonishing. The public sector worker would receive a pension of £28,900 compared with £11,600 for the private sector worker.

25% of council tax payments are used to fund public sector pensions – source Ros Altman – former government pension adviser.

Money magic.

The illusion starts with my daughter-in-law explaining how she got £300 worth of wine for "free".

Julia and I do not normally shop at Tesco, primarily since if time is worth spent physically shopping as distinct from on-line, then one might as well spend plenty of money. Therefore we go to Waitrose.

Nevertheless, having bought a new TV set on-line from Tesco due to the offer of a free installation of Sky (a deal pointed out to me by my son), we received "points" that themselves turned into vouchers with a value. We also got a little colourful booklet entitled "How to double up your vouchers on all this and more". Page 2 of the booklet explained a 4-stage process:-

Choose the department you want to spend your rewards tokens in.

Decide where you want to use your tokens (in-store, wine by the case, Tesco direct or grocery delivery charge).

Decide how many Clubcard vouchers you want to exchange.

Take your Clubcard vouchers to the Clubcard desk at your local store, where a customer service assistant will exchange them for double up rewards tokens.

"Make sure you don't go straight to the checkout as your vouchers cannot be doubled up there."

Seems simple enough if unduly complicated. The customer service assistant has a face glowing with rouge and bonhomie and explains that my £10 voucher can be doubled up – no problem there. My £5 voucher can be doubled up – no problem there. But, my £4 voucher cannot be because it is less than £5. Therefore she can turn £15 into £30's worth of rewards tokens and I can use the £4 just as a straight voucher discount, understand? Yes I think I have it and please proceed.

Clutching my 3 times £10 rewards tokens tightly in a sweaty hand (still thinking about what the customer service assistant will be doing after her shift ends) and putting the £4 voucher in a safe pocket, I proceed post haste to the wine section. What my daughter-in-law had explained is really true. There are shelves of wine at half price (that is how £300 worth was obtained with just £75 in vouchers – get it?). However, my eye is caught by a 3 bottles for £10 offer. Seems too good to miss and so I choose two separate white wines and grab 3 of each.

To insure against the 3 for £10 stuff not being up to quality standard, I then spot a marvellous New Zealand Marlborough that will have previously been priced "at some Tesco stores" at £9.99. It is now half-price at £4.99 (we can forgive the odd half-pence error). I go for 2 bottles thinking that I have more or less spent the £30 rewards tokens (6 bottles from 3 for £10 and 2 bottles at a fiver each).

About to leave the wine counter, I suddenly remember the £4 voucher. Nearly made a mistake. I grab thankfully a lovely Isla Negra Chilean Chardonnay at £3.99, half price. That should just about do it. On the way to the checkout I collect 4 large potatoes for tonight's steak dinner and a large jar of Nescafe coffee priced at £3. I enquire of the checkout assistant if she wants the rewards vouchers and the token before of after the checkout routine (must not make a mistake at this stage as I recall the threat note below the 4 options outlined in the booklet). She confirms "at the end" and wants my Tesco clubcard to award more points for this purchase basket. Amazing really. The net cost to me, and I have studied the till roll now for over half an hour and am still no wiser on how it happened, is £2.08. What I forgot to mention was that the jar of coffee is for our local village hall of which I am chairman. The £3 mentioned on the till roll will be reimbursed to me by the treasurer.

In conclusion, I bought from our local Tesco 9 bottles of good wine, 4 large potatoes and a large jar of coffee for -92p. Can anyone beat that? First thing Monday morning I intend to dump my Tesco shares on the basis that the purchase of a TV was a one-off, my wife will still shop at Waitrose and the world has gone completely and utterly mad.

Icelandic volcano eruption – an economic view.

Since they still owed us (UK) a cartload of cash,

they effected as payback a sky-load of ash.

We are stranded in Thailand

and cooling on Iceland,

vengeance for asset-freeze,

our economic trash?

Goldman Sachs – how does it work?

"If a picture paints a thousand words …" Today's Daily Telegraph has a wonderfully evocative picture of a fruit machine's reels spinning to stop on the revenue earned by Goldman Sachs as a 2010 first quarter estimate by "industry experts". As someone who used to be a senior director of the Bell-Fruit Group, I have sentimental memories of the cherries that are on the reels and that have nearly hit the pay line. Cherries are symbolic in the fruit-machine game. They usually give the biggest pay-out and are of course what we all want to pick. In this image, the Goldman Sachs money-making machine did not quite scrump the cherries but only because it has the orchard farmer on its tail. One other thing. Hidden deep in its software, the fruit-machine has a "compensator" that over a given cycle only allows the punter to win a given percentage of the "take." The rest goes to the house.

According to the estimates for the first quarter, the house took $11.1bn, paid out $5.5bn in pay and bonuses and still was left with a bottom line of $3.8bn (up 50%). The natives are getting restless. Some are digging deep into how the firm actually works and alleging something horrible in the woodshed:-

The US Securities and Exchange Commission (SEC) is prosecuting GS for alleged fraud in relation to its handling of collateralised debt obligation (CDO) instruments. Specifically, alleged untruths by a GS banker to professional investors.

The firm has been subpoenaed to hand over documents to the Lehman Brothers liquidator under suspicion that it was partly responsible for triggering the downfall by shorting Lehman stock.

A number of financial regulators around the world are investigating GS over alleged derivatives mis-selling including the German regulator and the European Union.

Gordon Brown, the UK prime minister, has announced an investigation by the FSA.

GS is being investigated for its role in helping Greece as a sovereign state to use accounting tricks to hide its debt pile. Chairman Gerald Corrigan has admitted that complex currency transactions were used in 2001 that "enabled politicians to mask borrowings."

So, how does the money-making machine work? As with the compensator in a fruit-machine, I have no idea. But someone does and when that someone has to talk and open files, we will all be the wiser, and happier?

All roads lead from Greece (and one thing leads to another).

We all know about Grecian tragedies but there has not been one like this before. After months and months of dithering, EU leaders "jaw-dropped" world markets by announcing a 750bn euros rescue package and coupled it with direct purchases of Greek, Portuguese and Spanish debt. Greece had been running a casino larger than the whole of Las Vegas and Reno together. Not only that, beaurocrats and non-tax-paying citizens had been betting against the house for seemingly ages with the help of an elusion performed by our friends at Goldman Sachs. That might work in the short term but it ends in tears. The house known as the big global market always wins in the end. And so it did with Greece that is well and truly a busted flush. (One leading Grecian economist claimed that 75,000 extra civil servants had been recruited in the last one year alone "When the ones we already have, have nothing to do").

Whether the monetary intention was sound or not (we can liken it to our own QE programme as inflation rises rapidly), the roads from Greece creep ever closer and the ripple effect becomes a tsunami. What is happening is that foreign (to Greece that is) holders of Greek and Portuguese debt have leapt on the intervention by the EU to exit their positions. This leaves the eurozone taxpayers exposed. This weakens the euro and makes exports to euroland more expensive and decreases demand in the market taking 60% of UK exports. The FTSE has dropped by over 12% in the time this tragedy has been unwinding and a new sovereign coin (banking on gold – the value of last resort) that fetched £164 a second or so ago, now cost £210. Very scary stuff and we all thought the credit crunch was bad. Quantitative easing to quantitative wheezing one might say.

The new UK coalition government is going to tighten our belt at last. Well it had better move real fast since Ireland, Greece, Portugal, Spain and now Italy are, inter alia, freezing public sector pay like a new ice-age has dawned. We are not in the EU monetary union but we sure are in the fiscal one. Our pension is starting to weep.

German shorting ban . Sorry but we understand not.

Our maverick friends in Germany have unilaterally introduced a ban on short selling of European Union government debt. The initial response by just about everyone that is not German (the consequence helps German exports) was outrage. The second response is "Sorry! – what?"

Paul Cluley, a partner at Allen & Overy said "There is a lot of confusion within BaFin (German market regulator) at what they have banned and what they haven't … It's clear that these rules came as almost as much surprise to them as to the rest of the market."

Andreas Schmitz, head of the German banking industry's lobbying group and of HSBC's business in Germany said, "If you close a market, another one will open elsewhere." Clemens Boersig, chairman of Deutsche Bank, added, "Policy makers should not do unilateral moves anymore."

We would all do well to remember. Union is one thing. Germany another.

Coalition – A Poem.

The clean-cut well-bred Englishmen
have risen to the fore,
Clear of eye, assured of voice
and of so square of jaw.
I'll trade your £10k of no tax
for my inheritance free,
but what I really want from you –
the senorita on my knee.

New macro-prudential regime.

This article has nothing to do with some cheap supermarket from the continent or the huge boo-boo dropped by our erstwhile esteemed insurance group chasing a far-eastern continent. But it is about a regime. More specifically a change of regime.

There was a body known as the FSA. It was full of nice chaps who had a lovely long sleep whilst Northern Rock glibly handed out 125% mortgages on the back of a fag packet and whilst the likes of HBOS purchased high-yielding wholesale bundles of debt that was not something it pretended to be. So, the new UK Coalition Government has decided to do away with the FSA, or rather, break it into bits and put most of it within the Bank of England for future safekeeping.

In simple layman terms, what is the objective for the economy? The answer is to attain a much more steady supply of credit. It might all take until 2012 and it might merely place the nice chaps in different slots but if that objective is achieved, it will have been worthwhile. Three cheers for the coalition. No need to read further. The rest, which sets out the new regime, is boring. Though not as boring as the FSA used to be.

* There will be a Prudential Regulator. Chaired by the Governor of the B of E, it will take over responsibility for supervising individual banks and other financial firms. The body will be a direct subsidiary of the B of E.

* A Consumer Protection and Markets Authority will be formed to regulate the conduct of every authorised financial firm providing services to consumers.

* The existing Monetary Policy Committee of the B of E will be twinned by a Financial Policy Committee that will have "the tools and the responsibility to look across the economy at the macro issues that may threaten economic and financial stability and the tools to take effective action in response."

* The crime attacking wing of the FSA will be merged with those of the Serious Fraud Office and the Office of Fair Trading. The target of the single policeman will be serious economic crime.

Objective – Retain AAA. Impediment – Soft underbelly.

Indigesting the chewy bits of UK Chancellor George Osborne's budget of 22nd June 010, it seems clear that the principal objective whether stated or not is the retention of the sovereign AAA credit rating. The big question though is this, does the nation have a collective square jaw comparative to that of the privileged-educated triumvirate of Cameron, Clegg and Osborne? If not, and if the soft underbelly of consumer man has grown too big to be starved, then will history repeat?

Andrew Marr's book The Making of Modern Britain has much to say about the "Goat" as Lloyd George was unaffectionately known. When he was Chancellor (before his elevation to PM) he cut real government consumption by 11%. It is generally held that this presaged the demise of the Liberal Party and started a sequence of events culminating in the General Strike of 1926. The relevance of this is that according to Martin Weale of the National Institute for Economic and Social Research, Osborne's proposed cut in the broadest measure of state activity is 10% by the year 2015. Could social unrest on a national scale happen again? Unlike the 1920's, today's generation are used to spending now and paying later. On the other hand they are better educated – more aware of the debt pile. But still …..

Markets have reacted well to the Budget. The yield on 10-year government bonds has fallen not least since the national debt should drop to about 69% of GDP from an otherwise 74.4%. Of course the cuts to the public sector and the rise in VAT to 20% in early January 011 could have been less to achieve the same end if certain taxes had not been reduced (such as the effect of a rise of £1k in the personal income tax allowance). Those, by the way, were the coalition's Liberal Party contributions. Sounds familiar?

G20 goes for banker.

Having written about the G20 (not to mention the G8) several times, I have finally cracked the code. "G" stands for globetrotters and 20 is the number of bottles of water the attendees must be seen to drink before the vino goes down. This time the top politicians met in Toronto and next November they zip over to Soul, perhaps since South Korea has just come third in an index of global competitiveness compiled by Deloitte and the US Council of Competitiveness.

The Toronto G20 agreed that in future banks must keep enough capital on their balance sheet to be able to withstand another 2008 style Lehman Brothers collapse. Under the present Basel 1 & 2 standard, banks must hold 8% of "safe capital". But this is what the final communiqué said, "the amount of capital will be significantly higher, and the quality of capital significantly improved, when the new rules are fully implemented. This will enable banks to withstand, without government support, stresses of the magnitude associated with the recent financial crisis". The consensus is that the 8% could rise to double figures but be vigorously contested by France and Germany whose banks traditionally hold less capital on their balance sheets than in the US or UK.

The focus on the French and German way of doing things is relevant, indeed the whole of

Europe is affected. The Bank of International Settlements (BIS) warned in its recently published annual report, "Ultra low rates and fiscal stimulus by governments is exacerbating matters, causing moral hazard and leading to the sort of zombie banks seen in Japan during its so-called Lost Decade. Such powerful measures have strong side-effects, and their dangers are becoming apparent. The time has come to ask how they can be phased out". This is all a bit non-G20 ish.

The economic argument is as old as the hills. Stimulate and risk rampant inflation. Self-flagellate and get depressed. My personal view stays as it has been throughout this crisis (tracked in Quantitative Wheezing ISBN 978-1-4466-6609-8), the consumer materialistic world had gone mad. It has to be reined in: not encouraged back to life.

Part 2

£2 trillion and counting.

Officially, UK public sector net debt is put at £932bn. But it could be £1.13 trillion higher. That is quite an error. Who says so?

That august body The Institute of Chartered Accountants in England and Wales (ICAEW) and the Centre for Economic and Business Research (CEBR) have got together and costed the off-balance sheet liabilities that the UK has clocked up. These include public sector pensions, public private partnerships and other private finance initiatives.

Michael Izza, the ICAEW chief executive, said that it is necessary to "…… create a culture of fiscal responsibility".You can say that again. If you came to me for a loan and told me your debt was currently X and I found it to be X times 2 and a bit, I sure would think about refusal or at best hike up the servicing cost of some more debt. Maybe those overseas buyers of our gilts will too.

From £7.99 to £1,600 in 35 years.

It seems that a man named Adam Fergusson, who was an adviser to the then UK Tory minister Lord Howe, wrote a book in 1975 called "When money dies". It is about how the German economy was ruined by hyperinflation after the Weimar government allowed public spending to run out of control. Copies of the book are reported to be changing hands at up to £1,600. Why? The answer supposedly is our friend the Sage of Omaha i.e. Warren Buffett. He is said to have told friends that this is precisely what could happen again if European governments attempt to spend their way out of the current recession.

Obviously the 1920's German experience will not recur since their present Chancellor has held firm, Gordon Brown has gone and the UK Coalition is putting the engine in reverse.

Still, at £1,600 a pop, somebody thinks there are lessons still to be learned.

Stand up and be counted.

Even in a democracy. Even with a change of Government. Even when your Coalition partner has to be listened to – there is still room for people to be told to toe the line. This is where the Select Committee of the House of Commons comes into its own.

It was the Treasury Select Committee that put Sir Fred Goodwin on the spot and cross-questioned the Governor of the B of E about quantitative easing and the like. Now this wonderfully maverick body has a new head in Andrew Tyrie. He was once chief economist at the European Bank of Reconstruction and Development and an economic adviser to John Major.

First in the griller will be the new Chancellor. He will be questioned on the doubted independence of the Office for Budget Responsibility (whose chairman Sir Alan Budd no sooner got his feet under the table than he resigned), on the content of the budget itself and on the forthcoming Comprehensive Spending Review.

I like the idea of this cross-party examination panel that seemingly has no-one but itself to answer to. We will monitor progress and feel the squirms.

Singapore is hot and steamy.

Every economist in the UK has been both surprised and amazed in an uptick of 1.1% in UK GDP in the quarter to end of June 010. Did it really happen? If it did, it was because builders started work again and factories re-started making things. It has to be said that during the months of April, May & June, the weather has been cool and not spectacular.

In Singapore by contrast it is always hot, very hot and sticky and spectacular. And so it proved to be for their economy too. Having taken a dive in the South China Sea and become a parking lot for the world's tanker fleet, suddenly the multi-cultural, super-clean Singapore scene is back on track with a recorded rise in GDP for the first half of 2010 registered at a colossal 18.1%. With a likely annual growth rate for 2010 of maybe 13% to 15%, even the mighty China could be surpassed.

My book "Barn door to balance sheet" ISBN 978-1-4461-1930-3 chronicles events in Singapore in the years 1972-1974 when, as a young management consultant working for Price Waterhouse, I worked on the merger of the telecommunications authorities (STB & TAS). So, Julia and I will add to one of the four drivers of the Singaporian economy (tourism) in October for a journey down sentimental road. I will write about how things have changed. One thing that hasn't is the heat and the steam – and I cannot wait.

Accommodation at the Bank of England.

Not of the bed-and-breakfast type (of which I have just had a bellyful having sweated through week 1 of Wainwright's Coast-to-Coast challenge walk) but of the "broadening asset" type.

The B of E only accepts securitised loans from individual banks and building societies as collateral security for using its discount window facility to borrow gilts.

After a three-month consultation period, this conservative category of securitised loans will be widened to include portfolios of loans to individuals and non-banks. The pay-back demanded will be greater transparency from lenders on the constitution of asset-backed securities and covered bonds. The objective is to allow more liquidity in the banking system but with greater transparency so that in the event of a default, the B of E is not left with its trousers down. That is to say, it has a good chance to sell on the securities received rather than having to take undue risk and demand expensive insurance against loss.

Credit crisis gone away and not return another day.

It's good news week – for the banking fraternity.

This was the week when the big UK listed banks (and all with global reach) reported a return to healthy profits. Following the crisis of the past two years, an overview of this phenomenon lacks any cynicism. A huge gasp of relief is more appropriate.

In this post-medicine era, even the evil high salaries and outlandish bonus payments can be viewed with a jaundiced approbation. Not once have I seen it reported that out of the pay-packet goes at least 52% to the exchequer – it can be more currently depending on the salary bracket of the recipient. On top, Mr UK taxpayer has recouped an estimated ten times the £500m expected to be taken from the special tax imposed by the last administration on individual bonuses higher that £25k. If one considers that this taxation is reparation and that the bankers themselves do not exactly salt their bread away for a rainy day, it has all helped oil the otherwise creaky wheels of commerce.

HSBC kicked off the week with a reported uptick profit of a 121% increase for the first six months of the year coming in at £7.1bn. The global banking and markets division made 50% of that figure emphasising the Far Eastern roots and indeed the boss man in now based in Hong Kong.

Next in line comes Barclays with a £3.95bn profit. The bank's investment banking arm produced £3.4bn of the total, an increase of 225%, again in the half-year. This "investment" gain had actually little to do with banking as such but rather a betterment of its own debt and a big reduction in impairments against troubled assets.

Standard Chartered, Lloyds Banking Group and RBS all followed suit to a lesser degree. In the latter case, the nationalised bank says it is on course to exit the government's Asset Protection Scheme in 2012.

What is good news for bankers, is good news for all of us.

UK national debt stands at 333% of GDP.

Just as you thought things were getting better, up pops The Institute of Economic Affairs (IEA) to calculate that the "real" UK national debt is £4.8 trillion or 333% of current GDP. The IEA seems to have been stung into life by data published this week from the Office for National Statistics (ONS).

The key criticism of what is deemed national debt is twofold. First, the ONS version (itself a record high figure) excludes the bank bail-outs and secondly omits the state's pension liabilities. It is not lost on the IEA that standard accounting practice would require the pension liability to be disclosed and added in.

Nick Silver, an IEA research fellow, said that the true figure should embrace £1.2 trillion of public sector pension liability and £2.7 trillion state pension liability. On the basis of the whole liability as calculated by the IEA, the true burden works out at £78,000 for every person in the UK. I rather doubt that the revellers at the Edinburgh festival this week knew or cared about their hidden burden and perhaps they are right. We used to say that ignorance is bliss. It looks like it will need to be for a generation or two. And by the way, why is petrol 5p a litre cheaper in Scotland than England.

USA deficit vacuum that isn't.

Nature hates a vacuum. And so it seems do the good people of America. According to ICI data, US citizens have invested a record $185bn into bond funds this calendar year (2010) and thus arguably finding the smartest investment category irrespective of whether monetary stimulus continues.

Where does the vacuum come in? The answer is the ever-approaching Sino-American clash. The Chinese establishment's jeering at America's credit worthiness has been implemented to the degree that, according to USA Treasury data, China has cut its holding of Treasury debt by $100bn over the past year or about 10%. The recycling of China's trade surplus and, consequently, the brake on the price of its currency, is being effected by purchasing sovereign bonds issued by Japan, Thailand, Latin America and by investing in commodities such as Timber in Guyana and shares in other commodity companies, for example, in Australia.

Perhaps it is in the nature of things that America's debt is coming home. Things have changed. Americans are saving again. Those surplus nations used to feeding off USA demand are going to have to go the Chinese route. Except that China is one heck of a competitor right now.

Mercantilists.

An earlier article concluded that those creditor sovereign nations that had accumulated their reserves by selling buckets loads of stuff to Americans were going to find times harder now that saving had become more powerful than spending to the average US citizen. A new word is in vogue to describe these suppliers, namely mercantilists. It is a beautifully generic term that renders unnecessary the spelling out of individual country names.

Under one proposal to get the US economy moving again, these mercantilists will face a further hurdle in the shape of a weaker greenback. A cheaper dollar makes imports more expensive. The proposal comes from our old friend Professor Tim Congdon of International Monetary Research. He says that the US market should be blitzed with bond purchases but out-with the banking system. A programme of the "right sort" of QE would expand M3 (the broadest measure of money supply) and stimulate the economy. The rationale is that banks sit on their new money whereas the likes of insurers, pension funds and Joe public do not. Specifically, Mr Congdon is reported as saying that $750bn of the right sort of QE would create a 5% rise in M3 in just three months and thus transform the economic outlook.

Congdon's solution seems unlikely to occur and so will not let the mercantilists off the hook, and nor will fiscal tightening that ought to accompany it, ala the UK model. The climate will continue to harden over the pond and will the non-New York, non-Californian natives get restless?

China's open and closed door.

You are welcome to come in but you cannot take our valuable stuff away.

That, very crudely, seems to be the current trading stance of the increasingly behemoth middle kingdom.

Xi Jinping, China's vice president and maybe president-in-waiting, told an investment forum that his country would be open to foreign companies carrying out state projects as part of its commitment to becoming one of the world's most attractive destinations for foreign investments. "With regard to government purchases and construction projects, the Chinese government will adopt an open, transparent plan to let foreign companies and technological products enjoy equal treatment". This statement is of course in response to Western companies voicing their disquiet at the way they are disadvantageously treated and once in China the lack of profitability as a result. It is noticeable that large entities such as Vodafone have pulled out of their Chinese joint ventures of late.

Rare earth minerals is the leading example of a closed door. Japan's foreign minister Katsuya Okada has issued what must be regarded as a formal protest to China saying that the sudden cessation of exports of these metals from China was "affecting the global production chain". According to a report in the Daily Telegraph,

Beijing set off shockwaves in July 010 when it announced a 72% reduction in rare earth exports. The point at issue is that China has acquired a near monopoly, with 97% of global output after under-cutting the rest of the world with Mongolian ores in the 1990's. The last US mine closed in 1996.

Apparently, rare earth minerals are not actually rare. There are ample supplies in the US, Australia, Canada, Russia and Greenland. But they are scattered about and costly to extract and a reliable global supple could take 15 years to re-develop. We are dealing with Neodymium and Cerium amongst others and does it matter? Well if you still want an iPad, Blackberry, plasma TV, laser, wind turbine, hybrid engine or smart bomb, it certainly does.

Whatever we make of China, one cannot accuse them of thinking short-term. Like playing chess against a good exponent, the consequences of early moves are only apparent as the checkmate looms.

Basel 111.

It is 22 years since regulators chose a beautiful Swiss town to lay down rules that, principally, were intended to force banks to maintain a level of balance sheet strength such that a financial firestorm would be avoided. As we all know only too well, in October 08 (read Quantitative Wheezing for a blow-by-blow account), the banking system did indeed run out of liquidity and so proving that the early day rules were inadequate, out of time or just plain bypassed.

Now, precisely 13th September 010, financial regulators have reached a new deal intended to force the huge and global-reach banks to double the spare cash they hold. Such a dramatic escalation in "insurance" might have been expected to damage financial markets. In the event it did not. There are probably two main reasons for this:-

*The push for higher reserves had been widely foreseen and

* Phasing-in will take place gradually between 2015 and 2018.

Whilst the implementation period might seen an act of procrastination, Angela Knight, chief executive of the British Bankers' Association, explained it this way, "The transition is the critical bit as the rules take money out of the economy. Even though the UK banks are in a much stronger place than most on capital, the Basel changes need to be implemented over a long time-table and very carefully sequenced to avoid prolonging the downturn".

The new rules, called Basel 111, demand that banks hold 4.5% of common equity and retained earnings. This so called Tier 1 ratio currently stands at 2%. Secondly (and as a direct response to the outcry of feast and famine cycles) there must be an additional buffer of 2.5% to be accumulated in good times. Such a buffer can be used in a time of need but only at the cost of restricting dividends.

Overall, premeditated, studied and sensible.

Forget being NICE, get SOBER.

The one man we have come to rely on to steady the ship through the storm of the credit crisis has developed a penchant for acronyms. Mervyn King, Governor of the Bank of England, believes we in the UK have left behind a decade of being NICE. This was the ten years of "Non-Inflationary Consistently Expansionary" economic activity. But the credit crisis killed all that stuff off. One might say (to paraphrase his words speaking at the Black Country Chamber of Commerce – no pun intended) that any expansionary binge will cause a hangover to last for quite some time.

It follows logically, according to Mr King, that over the next decade we have to SOBER up. That is to say we must Save, have Orderly Budgets and exercise Equitable Rebalancing. Contrived it might be, but the reasoning is sound. Listen to the wise man, "The counterpart of strong consumption was low saving. Having averaged close to 20% in the 1960's and 1970's, gross national savings fell to just 12% of income in 2009 – the lowest since the war. This was all the more remarkable because one might have expected saving to increase as life expectancy rose. In the coming years, we will have to save more". He went on, "We need to sell more to, and buy less from, economies overseas".

The overall theme of the acronyms is that deficit countries such as the UK must consume less of what is made in (say) China and surplus counties must rely less on exports. The sting in the tail is of course international accord. Should self-interest prevail or corrections occur too quickly at too great a degree then there is a real danger of a collapse of activity all round.

Another month, another record debt.

Guy Fawkes might well be drifting further into the background but UK debt continues to sky-rocket. The lecture by the Governor of the B of E to SOBER up might equally well be addressed UK Public Body & Co Ltd.

Public sector net borrowing hit £15.6bn in September 010, the highest on record and 5.4% up year-on-year. Total UK debt at the end of September was £953bn (source, Office for National Statistics) being 64.6% of GDP. This debt firework is equivalent to £15,000 for each UK resident. The debt trap that many private individuals are only too aware of can be illustrated by the fact that the UK's tax revenue actually increased (let's say your salary) but interest payments increased by more (say your credit card interest). This is the downward spiral that only urgent pruning can arrest. Technically,

the higher national interest was caused by interest payments on index-linked gilts plus the quantum of greater overall debt.

The UK Chancellor, George Osborne, referred to the debt as a "supertanker" using the analogy to picture the effort to stop never mind draw back the beast from its momentum. Without wishing to sound flippant, it is a few supertankers of stuff from China that need turning back; as a start.

Bring back UK GAAP.

Nigel Lawson (ok, we all prefer Nigella) was by most reckoning a good Chancellor of the Exchequer. That though was a while ago. Now as Lord Lawson and in his capacity as sitting on the House of Lords Economic Affairs Committee he is quoted as saying, "I think we need UK GAAP (Generally Accepted Accounting Principles) back because London is a financial centre because it has a competitive advantage in a legal framework and a trustworthy information framework of accounting standards. For some reason we decided (in 2005) to go for the international standards, which is potentially a race to the bottom."

What the ex-chancellor is talking about is the introduction of IFRS (International Financial Reporting Standards) which many think disguise the build-up of risks in banks. Tim Bush, a city veteran, gave evidence to the "Urgent Issues Task Force" saying that unwittingly in relation to banks, IFRS "produced false profits and over-stated capital" which had "misled creditors, misled shareholders, the Bank of England, the Financial Services Authority and others."

At the heart of this ire is that the IFRS exclude the need for bad debt provisioning, distort bank's company accounts, and so give false assurances that in turn hamper directors and regulators from seeing the build up of leverage and other risks. Mr Bush reasoned that previously UK company law was attached to investigation departments and had worked out all the ruses people had got up to in accounting over 100 years and so had build safeguards into the law of the land.

We want our GAAP back.

More money printing in USA.

UK stock market loves it, quite a few economic commentators hate it, but whatever, the US Federal Reserve has taken the big decision to place a further $600bn of new money into the economy adding to the $1.7 trillion already actioned. There is however a difference in this tranche regarding what it is to purchase with the new greenbacks. Hitherto, corporate debt and mortgage-backed securities were bought. This time it is government bonds. Ironic in that in so doing it apes the UK practice on the day that the Monetary Policy Committee of the B of E decided not to pump more dosh into the economy.

Interest rates were held at 0% to 0.25% as since December 08 and this is where most criticism relates since it is the weakening of the dollar that non-Americans are raging about. It can be viewed as a form of monetary protectionism in the face of China holding out against tightening its currency. Furthermore, the US dollar is the world's reserve currency meaning that, inter alia, it can borrow from the rest of the world in its own currency. It is argued that each time the Fed prints money it devalues that debt. Lenders are obviously on the other end of this devaluation and this helps explain why for example China has been selling off its US dollar stockpile.

With a stubborn 10% of the available workforce unemployed, the US position is understandable but as the Governor of the B of E has said, actually the big boys have to work together and not in isolation. Odds are that Japan and not China will be the first to retaliate in this monetary war of the worlds.

Half way to paradise.

You will not read this anywhere else. After a self-conducted, self funded and wholly scientific survey, I can report with absolute confidence that the UK is exactly half way to regaining the economic position held just prior to the collapse of Lehman Brothers in September 08.

Yesterday a self-employed, one-man-band electrician did a couple of jobs at our house. Before leaving I asked if the credit crisis had impacted his business. Yes it had but he had stuck it out and things were improving. "This is how I measure it. My wholesale supplier delivers once a week. Before all this happened, he used to arrive at 4.30 in the afternoon. At the worst point last year he was arriving at 10.30 in the morning. Now he turns up at about 1.30 pm".

Since I am extremely good at arithmetic, I calculate that this means the wholesale supply chain in half way back to complete recovery. One final aside, as he jumped into his cab he said, "Another thing, when there is a bit of gloomy news on the radio or tele', my 'phone stops ringing for two days. Then it starts again".

So there we have it. Half way to paradise.

Ireland's knock-out and knock-on.

Notwithstanding the placatory statements from Irish politicians, Ireland has agreed a loan of between 80 to 90 billion euros. This loan is intended to be used to recapitalise its banks and provide a contingency fund against government borrowing. Thus, the Emerald Isle becomes the second EU country to capitulate after Greece.

It is ironic that whilst the Greeks experienced relative stability once its rescue was in place (though there was, and continues to be, public unrest and some rioting), the announced rescue of Ireland has been heralded by chaos. Chaos mostly due to the Green Party who are a minority partner in the ruling coalition. They, plus a few independent members of the Irish parliament, are threatening to call a general election in January 011. This uncertain political climate has all the makings of a self-inflicted knock-out blow.

The point about the affects of jitters across Europe is that spooking the financial markets is having a knock-on to the deemed next weakest brethren of Portugal and Spain. Portugal is already in the throes of a general strike and politicians in Madrid are watching events very carefully.

The Irish rescue package involves the EU, the IMF and, to the consternation of many this side the Irish sea, the UK and Sweden. This offered help from the UK is not altruistic. UK based banks are heavily into Irish loans and sovereign gilts and not least the nationalised Lloyds Banking Group. The best indicator of market concern is that the benchmark Irish 10-year government debt rose 1.5 basic points to 7.99% and the cost of insuring 5-year debt rose 25 basic points to 5.3%. These are interest costs close to a debt trap in which only default remains an option.

The book Quantitative Wheezing tracked the crisis engulfing Ireland in the period October 08 through to March 010 along with other major world credit crisis developments. But the knock-out and knock-on of the Irish economy is still as much a dreaded realisation as it is sad.

Come back British Railways, all is forgiven.

Sir Roy McNulty has produced an interim report on the value for money of the UK railway network. In it he claims to have found "substantial scope for change" based upon costs that have risen from a taxpayer contribution of £2.3bn in 1993/4 to £5.2bn in 2008/9, that is to say, since privatisation.

The current Transport Secretary (none of this breed last too long in office) Philip Hammond said that he would establish a "high-level group" to "consider options for structural reforms in the industry" – this is thought to be code for experimenting with "vertical integration" on the network such that, say, a single operator may run both the actual trains and the track itself.

Does anyone remember British Railways? Does anyone remember the professional fees and associated costs of splitting the train from its track from its financing/leasing arm from the signalling and stations and car parks? Does anyone remember when a railway was thought of as a composite business entity? Of course Indians and Chinese were not bright enough to engineer a split up of a railway system and they carried on in the same old way that will probably be a key recommendation of the "high-level group".

What goes round, comes around, as they say. Even round railway wheels.

Worry beads.

A string of miniature worry beads did not, as I had anticipated, burst from my Christmas cracker. Nevertheless, worry beads are a Christmas cracker for the dying days of 2010. The use of worry beads is as old as human history and, using modern day parlance, their primary purpose is to absorb negative energy. Negative energy absolutely oozed from the crystal ball lying in the toe of the Christmas stocking. A crystal ball that threatened to reveal the economic parameters for 2011.

The very first entry in my credit crunch diary (Quantitative Wheezing ISBN 978-1-4466-6609-8) dated 7th October 2008 discussed the UK bank rate with the words, "It has been kept so long at 5% as the principal weapon against the fear of rising inflation". Regular readers of my diary and indeed every single saver in the land will know that the UK bank base rate has been at an historical low of 0.5% since March 2009. Which leads to the first worry bead flipping from hand to hand. Paul Fisher, the Bank of England's director of markets, is reported as saying that the base rate will soon rise eventually "normalising" close to 5%. That is one hell of a consequential prediction heightened by the impression that the "eventual" bit probably means during 2011. The point is that if the UK faces an early rise in bank rate, it will come when, inter alia:-

*British households have £1,200bn of mortgage debt.

*Two thirds of borrowers are on variable repayment rates.

*UK growth is extremely sensitive to higher borrowing rates.

*During November 2010, the Government borrowed £23.3bn being the highest total in a single month since records began.

*UK Government spending is running at about 11% higher than tax receipts.

* UK inflation has been running above the B of E's target of 2% for 40 out of the last 49 months and indeed over the past few months the RPI measure has been over 5%.

And so a macro look at the negative energy edging towards 2011 is positively gloomy and this is before we think about rising oil prices (household oil now at 72p a litre – 50% up on just a month ago), rising utility bills generally and the higher sterling cost of imported food stuffs. If one does not want to fidget further with the worry beads, try not to think about eurozone debt. Just try not.

A highly disaggregated bottom-up process.

Look; stop laughing, lift back up your jaw and absolutely no rude rejoinder. This is a most serious business. The business of feeding to this UK Government those forecasts on which the most vital fiscal decisions may be based.

You can recall that one of the first moves of Gordon Brown was to make the Bank of England independent of the Treasury in, inter alia, setting interest rates via a new Monetary Policy Committee (some claim on the advice of Mr Balls the now shadow Chancellor). It was only a matter of time before a new administration needed to demonstrate that it too could set up an "independent" body (this time a sort of watchdog) to have the final say on economic forecasting.

The new august body was called the Office for Budget Responsibility (OBR) and I am indebted to Philip Aldrick writing in the Daily Telegraph for unearthing the outcome of the pledge of transparency by obtaining this clarity from the OBR "a highly disaggregated bottom-up process". This process goes, apparently, something like this:-

*OBR produces a draft economic forecast.

*This forecast is sent to the Treasury, HM Revenue & Customs and The   Department for Work & Pensions.

*New figures for the forecast emerge from this referral.

*The circulation process iterates several times.

*Each feedback to the OBR is scrutinised and challenged.

* Judgements and assumptions are input by the OBR to give consistency.

*The final OBR forecast and resultant fiscal forecasts converge.

* The result is a submission of the economic forecast to the Government.

It is just amazing how sophisticated things can get. The head of my OBR is, and has been for some time now, my wife. Having regard to our joint income, she decides what we can afford to spend.

Turning their back on the Emerald Isle.

Buried somewhere deep inside my book Quantitative Wheezing is a diary entry called "Irish eyes not smiling". It represented one of the earliest indications that the credit crisis had reached beautiful Ireland. And it was more than just a factual thing; it was a surprise. A surprise since over the past couple of decades Ireland had become known as the Celtic Tiger where, as the prime examples, the best software engineers were moving to and the staggers drank the Liffey dry of Guinness and a Mr O'Leary was building a budget airline soon to surpass British Airways in the number of people flown around the rest of Euroland. Farmers got rich and property prices boomed. For the first time in Irish history, those born there could think about working there (there is much irony in that my book "Derbyshire born" refers to the Irish navvies that dug the huge channels needed to flatten out a track to carry the new Great Central Railway as it passed en-route London to Edinburgh in the late nineteenth century).

But now the Irish leave their homeland again. Not labourers but young graduates heading for Australia, New Zealand and Canada. According to a report by the Economic and Social Research Institute (ESRI), as many as 100,000 people will abandon Ireland by April 2012. The causal factors are reported as high unemployment (in the age group 20-24 year olds it is 31.7% for males and 19.3% for females), rising taxation and unhappiness generally with fiscal austerity.

The Irish lament is particularly poignant given that exports are forecast to rise by 6% this year. The sad fact is that legacy debt from those so called boom years and a current budget deficit running at 9.6%, are just too big to counter. Yet they will weep when they think back and hear again The Londonderry Air and Danny Boy vowing to take his Kathleen back "as tears come in your loving eyes".

So how is the FTSE doing?

On this last day of the first month of the new year, actually how is the UK top 100 company index doing?

This morning it stands at 5,848 so that does represent a set-back and not surprising given the upheaval in Egypt hard on the heals of Tunisia, the continuing uncertainty on financing the sovereign debts of Europe and the ditherings of Davos. But, putting all that to one side, two weeks ago this premier index reached 6,056 which was a 31 month high and in fact stretching back till just before the credit crunch started. More remarkable still is that from a nadir reached in March 09, the FTSE had risen by 72%.

The big question for investors and fund managers tracking the index is does late January 011 signify that the forward momentum is over or is it merely a temporary set back pending (say) corporates releasing their cash reserves to expand? There were optimists (bulls) forecasting an index rise to 7,000 by the close of this year. I prefer their camp and will act accordingly.

Old Japan and older Japanese.

For a long time Japan had the world's second largest economy. Not any more if official statistics are accurate. It has been shunted into third spot by China. The two old-world nations have one thing in common aside from a history of warmongering. Oldness. As we all know, the Chinese economy continues to grow rapidly but that of Japan does not. According to Takahora Ogawa, Standard & Poor's (S&P) Asian analyst, Japan's economy is the same size today in nominal terms as it was in 1992. However, public debt has tripled to reach a calculated 233% of GDP and 259% if bonds issued under the Fiscal Investment and Loan Programme are included. It is reported that Japan has not started to constrain credit and will have a budget deficit of 8% of GDP until at least 2013. Mr Ogawa said, "This is not affordable, Japan is running out of the domestic financial assets to absorb the debt".

S&P has cut Japan's $10.6 trillion debt by a notch to AA- that in itself will increase the interest debt burden.

Demographics are against Japan. Japan's Social Security Research Institute points out that the population has been contracting since 2005 and is forecast to fall from 127.5m to 89.9m by 2055. Already its median age is 44.4 years, a world record, and it is rising fast. What will surprise many people is that Japan is perceived as a wealthy nation and indeed it is the world's top external creditor having $3 trillion of net assets abroad. But the problem is like any big company or indeed individual in that if you cannot meet day-to-day financial requirements then your debts will have to be turned into cash to meet your creditors. If large sums are repatriated back to Japan, it could presage a fall worldwide in asset prices.

Japan is a long way off geographically. The message is that its problem with a shrinking workforce and old stagers is a fate that faces much of Europe too – not to mention China.

Caterpillar crawls uphill.

My recently published book Barn door to balance sheet (ISBN 978-1-4461-1930-3) contains a description of management consultancy work done by Price Waterhouse for Fiat-Allis, the then premier UK/Italian manufacturer of heavy-duty four-wheel loaders (the sort of meg-machines one sees pushing soil around when new roads are under construction). This is mentioned because at the time the big competitor in that market was the US firm Caterpillar. Since then Caterpillar has gone from strength to strength to become the largest manufacturer of construction and mining machinery in the world.

The context of Cat's recently expressed optimism of global economic recovery is that, according to the US's Institute of Supply Management's (ISM) index of the US manufacturing sector, new orders in January 011 surged to their highest level since early 2004. It is worth recalling that the UK Chancellor blamed the bad weather for the slight contraction in UK GDP recorded for the final quarter of 2010. Whilst the weather was bad across Great Britain at that time, it could hardly be compared with the snow that hit Central and North East US in the same January of this surged index. So why the contrast? Many economists will attribute the US increase in manufacturing activity to our old friend quantitative easing that has given the US a new dose of money supply. Plus, the Federal Reserve has brought in a $858bn tax cutting programme. Money supply pump-priming has stopped in the UK and taxes are on the increase. Maybe only the future rate of inflation each side of the pond will make the judgement.

What is interesting in the new world order of things is that manufacturing as a whole accounts for only 11% of the US's GDP (UK it is 13%) so the high ticket items from the likes of Cat assuage, at least in part, the continuing dominance of Chinese manufacturers.

Inflation to deflate growth prospects.

Best to forget the official B of E target rate for inflation of 2% since the UK is no nearer that bulls-eye than hitting the wire above the double twenty on a dartboard. The Office of National Statistics (ONS) has today issued its inflation figure for January 011. The 12 month % change is CPI 4.0% and RPI 5.1%.

According to the ONS, the five drivers of inflation between December 010 and January 011 were fuel and lubricants (due to the increase in VAT to 20% and the price of crude oil, petrol stood at £1.27 per litre, a record high), restaurants and cafes up 1.4% equalling the monthly record, alcoholic beverages up 6.7% (a monthly record), furniture and furnishings and the purchase of vehicles.

One could say that the national price for higher prices is higher credit charges. The yield on 10 year gilts has gone up 0.5% since the first of January 011 and a full 1% since September 010 to stand at 3.87%. We now know that total UK debt has not yet started to fall notwithstanding the Government's austerity drive and that the gap between the value of imports and exports is at its highest ever. We can now pile on that the greater cost of new debt to finance this deficit.

Meantime, over the pond, President Obama wants $7.2 trillion of new deficit spending over the next ten years as his quantitative easing programme continues. Latest figures say that China (the new world No 2 economic power), Japan and a few other foreigners now finance 40% of American debt.

In the increasing Western World of inflation, it is hard to see where new net growth is coming from aside from growth in the share of us taken by China.

Swiss coco at bedtime.

Several examples exist of the Gnomes of Zurich bending over backwards to accommodate/appease the new world order of banking regulation. Erstwhile secret accounts have been opened up to the US tax inspectors and Switzerland was the quickest off the blocks to freeze ex-President Mubarak's financial assets. In one other regard, the pendulum on the Swiss cuckoo clock has swung to almost the other extreme from secrecy.

Switzerland is demanding that its banks increase their capital ratios to a whopping 19% compared to the G7 demand for 7%. Such a reserve fund can be made up of equities (of course) but also (and before bedtime) coco's. Readers will recall that a new financial instrument has been invented called "contingent convertibles" (coco's). The contingent bit triggers with deep survival risk and the convertible bit is to equities. Coco's are bonds but they switch to risk capital if the issuing bank gets into trouble. The first test of the market's willingness to buy coco's is an issue valued at £3.9bn by Credit Suisse. The coupon is a remarkable 9%. An explanation for such a high return is the label of "death spiral convertibles" because holders such as pension funds and insurance companies may be forced sellers if conversion breached the total equity share of their total portfolio.

Matt Czepliewicz, an analyst at Collins Stewart said, "It places Credit Suisse ahead of the pack in meeting capital requirements and in developing this new segment of the European bank capital market".

Nuclear rock-ya baby.

Oh dear – of what can happen to financial markets in just six days. And, in the aftermath of the massive earthquake off the Japanese East coast on 10th March 011, it seems churlish to even think of money things when so many lives have been lost and lifestyles devastated. Even so, markets have been rocked and probably as much by the threat of nuclear radiation as by the Richter Scale 9.0 quake and resultant tsunami.

Yesterday (15th March) more than $1trillion was wiped off the value of stockmarkets worldwide as near panic of another financial global crisis spread. The Japanese Nikkei share index fell 10.6% taking losses to 16.3% over two consecutive days. This represents the biggest fall since 1987 and the third worst in history. Whilst the risk of increasing radioactive contamination from the Fukushima Daiichi complex has led, one might add inevitably, to a rush by investors to the "safety" of cash and bonds, empathy must lie with the president of the Tokyo Stock Exchange, Atsushi Saito, "I would appreciate it if all investors and trading participants would respond in a calm and orderly manner". It goes without saying though that for Japan and increasingly the global community, the fear of radiation is not amenable to calmness and orderliness.

In many ways it is almost as if Armageddon has been heralded. The world starts to recover from the credit crisis of 08-09 (read Quantitative Wheezing) to run slap bang into the geopolitical turbulence of the Middle East and North Africa. To appreciate the global reach of the Japanese crisis, these are the losses on the main Western markets yesterday:-

UK 1.38%

Germany 3.19%

France 3.90%

USA 2.00% (at opening on Wall Street).

Pension funds in the UK and hedge funds have suffered heavy losses not least because in the recent past it was believed that Japanese equities were good value and the weakened yen would stimulate Japanese exports. That in turn arose from the parlance state of the Japanese economy before the natural disasters with national debt standing at about 225% of GDP.

Will there be an instant dead-cat bounce? At the time of writing this article the FTSE 100 is down a further 0.85%. Conclusion – wherever you happen to be, Japanese nuclear will rock-ya baby.

Japan – the world's biggest creditor nation.

At a time when Japan's:-

* Public debt is 225% of its GDP.

* Tax revenue covers less than half its annual budget.

* Pension funds are net sellers of bonds to meet payments to the elderly.

* Central Bank has pumped 21 trillion yen (£168bn) into the economy.

* Central Bank has doubled its bond purchases to 10 trillion yen,

it beggars belief that here is a nation having about £2 trillion worth of net assets overseas and so making it the world's top creditor. It is all caused by the ingrained savings habit of its hard-working citizens and the use of "carry trade" whereby Japanese institutional investors such as insurance funds plus masses of individual people chased overseas asset yields when interests rates at home were at zero. We are talking US municipal bonds, commodity funds and, not least, UK equities.

What of it, one might think. The pull-back to Japan of overseas investments coupled with the failure to buy the debt issued by, for example, Australia, South Africa and Brazil, inevitably must lead to lower pricing of these overseas assets and debts. It follows that whilst the loss of output caused by the latest earthquake/tsunami/nuclear disasters hits Japan's domestic economy, the retrenchment of this creditor nation impacts the world's economy.

Pay-back time.

Through the medium of the Special Liquidity Scheme (see ISBN 978-1-4466-6609-8) the Bank of England provided £185bn of rescue funding to the UK's resident banks. The whole tenure was three years and the last repayment must be made by January 2012. The fund was not to be extended under any circumstances.

With ten months left to meet the termination deadline, lenders had repaid £94bn or 50.8%. The central bank does not say whether this progress is deemed satisfactory but something somewhere is working. Light at the end of a long, long tunnel?

Fidd'le-de-dee, and strike a light for me.

In my latest Financial Guide "How to wise-up on business & finance" – 978-1-4466-2195-0, I poke mild fun at any notion that accounting language, profit & loss accounts or indeed the venerable balance sheet is scientific in the sense of portraying truth.

Ofgem is the regulator guarding the consumer's interest in energy supply. According to Ofgem's latest report, the big six suppliers of gas and electricity seem to be making 38% or so more money from their customers than the accounts show.

My little book uses light-weight examples such as "dodgy balance" and a butcher's profit from selling his meat to demonstrate a principle. The UK energy suppliers are suspected of more heavy-weight treatment to put certain principles into practice. It appears likely (so Ofgem say) that the suppliers made £3bn from their UK supply and generation business and not the £2.2bn earnings before interest and tax as declared. "Exceptional items" is the favourite slot for a few largish numbers and RWE in particular spread £213m across different headings. Scottish and Southern were particularly creative in placing £127m as "portfolio optimisation". The only big player who did not engage in fiddley games was Centrica.

One hopes that the "independent firm of accountants" now appointed to examine the accounts of the big six were a few megawatts or light years distant from those signing off such accounts.

Ireland – in Last Chance Saloon?

It might be the understatement of the aftermath period of the great credit crisis to say that these are interesting times for Ireland and its banks.

On 20th April 2009, I wrote an article called "Irish eyes not smiling" and since then have periodically tracked the demise of the Irish economy with no little sentiment or altruistic anxiety. In the former case due to deep-rooted love of the Emerald Isle and in the latter caused by strong economic ties. Southern Ireland remains a major export market for the UK and the Lloyds Banking Group and RBS are among the biggest foreign banking creditors. It follows that if the latest efforts to pull Ireland from the brink of financial ruin fail, then the UK backers face billions of pounds of losses. So what are these latest efforts?

Patrick Honohan, governor of the Central Bank of Ireland, described the latest steps to save the Irish economy as "exceptional". The decision taken in October 2008 to guarantee all banks' debts and deposits left the Irish taxpayers with liabilities equal to 800% of the country's GDP. The European Central Bank's accounts for 2010 show that the Central Bank of Ireland owes 146bn euros. This, as it happens, is half as much again as Portugal, itself the subject of much financial hand-ringing in recent days.

Consequent to the central borrowings from Europe was the effective nationalisation of the three big banks namely Allied Irish Banks, Bank of Ireland and Anglo Irish Bank. Now the last chance saloon is one big bar in Dublin where Guinness is just too frothy to get drunk on.

Part 3

Bad, yet not so bad.

We all remember the old style building societies being divided into so-called "good" and "bad" banks as part of the process of rescue in the dark days of 2008. Now, according to a piece by Jamie Dunkley in the Daily Telegraph, some rather strange movement is taking place. On the one hand, the "good" bits of ex Northern Rock BS reported a loss of £232m in its latest accounts yet is being courted by the Coventry BS. Conversely, the "bad" bank holding the toxic assets of ex Northern Rock and ex Bradford & Bingley has returned to profitability. The figures reported by UK Asset Resolution (UKAR), which holds these businesses, and for the latest year were:-

• Northern Rock a profit of £200.1m.

• Bradford & Bingley a profit of £277.4m.

Two outcomes from the change of fortune of the bad firms are said to be that £1.1bn has been repaid off the Government loans and secondly UKAR plans to invest (wait for it) £68m in technology and processes to save £40m a year costs.

To give a modicum of perspective to this turnaround, UKAR still has a £110bn balance sheet and the taxpayer is still owed £21.7bn from the bad ex Northern Rock assets alone. Still, it seems the bad is not so bad.

Always look on the bright side.

Oh, doom-monger do thy worst. Triggered by the OECD's latest forecast that the UK economy will grow by only 1% over the next three months plus the fiscal tightening from yesterday's new UK tax year start, the doom-mongers are at it again. The headline retail sales "catastrophe" of stagnant sales means we are all destined for the workhouse.

But wait:-

• 1% is 1%. Given the size of the UK economy, actually it's quite a lot.

• The budget year 11/12, just started, increases the tax personal allowance by £1,000. It puts £200 into the pocket/purse of a lot of people who, almost by definition, are spenders and not savers.

• Retail sales are virtually useless since most of the stuff is imported. Value-added is what is needed.

• UK manufacturers are doing ok helped not a little by our Indian friends owing the likes of Jaguar cars.

• Most important of all, 75% of the UK's GDP is from the services side. There we are doing very well and it is highly skilled work by the brain boxes not shelf-fillers.

Always look on the bright side. And, by the way, get back into equities.

What is £3trillion in cash?

• A number using an awful lot of noughts.

• A figure equivalent to 8% of the world economy.

• The amount of cash (quantitative easing) that the world's central banks have pumped into the global financial system since the credit crisis began.

These figures are quoted in the Daily Telegraph as from Fathom Consulting were obtained by measuring the liquidity injections made by the world's four major central banks. The methodology was to measure how their balance sheet changed from prior to post the crisis. The banks were the US Federal Reserve, the European Central Bank, the Bank of Japan and the Bank of England and the combined reserves increased from $4trillion at the start of 2006 to just short of $9trillion ($5trillion being about £3trillion) by the end of February 2011. What is perhaps surprising is that of the four biggies, the Bank of England was the smallest player at £200bn whilst the European Central Bank was the largest.

What point is being made by this analysis? It is that this massive injection of liquidity is the main driver of stock markets rather than global corporate health. If it is, then it begs the question of what will happen to equity prices when QE starts to be reversed. This is a real and not theoretical worry not least since the huge scale of extra liquidity does not appear to have stimulated inflation via purchasing power nor gone into greater business investment. It must have gone somewhere and equities and corporate bonds seem the logical home.

New financial regulation – the grand plan.

It is just one year since the UK Chancellor included in his speech at the Mansion House, "No one was controlling levels of debt, and when the crunch came no one knew who was in charge".

Soon, that same Chancellor will tell Parliament what the grand plan is to fix things regulatory. The FSA (the big idea of the last holder of this august body) will be abolished with its powers transferred back to the Bank of England. Then, the establishment of three new regulatory bodies:-

• Financial Policy Committee (FPC). This committee will be charged with ensuring financial stability. Specifically, it will monitor the broader risks in financial markets whilst identifying excesses and vulnerabilities. The objective is to plug the supervisory gap apparent from the inquest on the credit crunch crisis and precisely as spoken by the new Chancellor. The committee will be chaired by the Governor of the Bank of England and housed within the bank.

• Prudential Regulation Authority (PRA). The PRA will assume the responsibilities of the soon to be defunct FSA for prudential regulation, that is to say, making sure banks have enough liquidity and base capital to withstand future shocks by relying on these resources alone. This authority will have as its single responsibility the promotion of financial stability of the whole UK financial system. It must be apparent that businesses in trouble can fail without the help of taxpayers or destabilising the broader markets and hence the link to the FPC. The authority will be a new division of the Bank of England.

• Financial Conduct Authority (FCA). The FCA will be in charge of enforcement and conduct and as such will inherit the more high profile role of the old FSA. Competition is seen as a key focus with the power to oversee the design of financial products, standards of placement of products and be able to ban products for up to a year. It can force firms to change or withdraw financial product promotions. A short-form title might be thought of as "consumer protection".

Ireland's 80%-90% write-off.

Previous articles have chronicled the growing economic crisis in Ireland. What goes up, must come down. And this time it's the turn of the subordinated debtors of Bank of Ireland. These unfortunate backers of the state of Ireland are to have their Tier 1 and Tier 2 securities bought back for just 10% and 20% respectively of the face value.

In total, the subordinated debt of this one bank (albeit Ireland's largest) was worth 2.6bn euros but new capital targets set by the government means that 5.2bn euros has to be raised before the end of July 011 in an attempt to protect the financial services industry from the ongoing crisis. This so-called haircut is not unexpected by the market and all junior debt in all banks and building societies has been trading at a fraction of its par value.

Is this a harbinger of things to come for the rest of the peripheral European states? Our maverick friends in Germany appear to be changing their tune on balking against a second tranche of aid for Greece and maybe this Irish example is why. German banks are known to hold much of Greece's government stock, not to mention the holdings in Portuguese and Spanish paper. We shall see, but certainly the junior debt of the smaller European states was not one for the balanced portfolio.

UK Quantitative Easing round 2 – by default.

It has been observed that the UK Government has managed to fund its continuing budget deficit, and at a low interest rate, due to the purchase of its debt by banks and building societies. Simon Ward, chief economist at Henderson Global Investors has said that these purchases are tantamount to a second round of quantitative easing. In other words, instead of the Bank of England printing money first-hand, it has done so second-hand, so to speak.

The sums involved are staggering in that over the past six months, banks bought £36.1bn or 91% of all gilts issued. As a comparator, the previous six month figure was £11.4bn. The compensatory drop in purchases of UK gilts by overseas buyers is thought to be due to less capital leaving the peripheral European economies for UK shores (see the article on Ireland's haircutting of junior debt).

Perhaps this pattern emerging of Europeans having the confidence to stay with their own debt is a turning point in the angst of the EU monetary crisis. Or maybe just coincidence. Either way, UK debt has found a home again – at home.

Greece will not default.

All the informed commentators agree that our maverick friends in Germany have made a rapid retreat in the face of the joint forces of France and the European Central Bank. Doesn't sound too plausible but maybe as likely as Greece not defaulting on its debts? What's it all about?

Germany, led by the country's finance minister Wolfgang Schauble, has been consistently and stubbornly demanding that holders of Greek bonds should be forced to share the costs of bailing out the sovereign state and in particular the banks which bought billions of euros of this Greek debt. One slight problem with that approach is that French banks are reckoned to hold 47.5% of Greece's debt of 103bn euros. Nasty. This would amount to a debt default whereas if creditors would agree to roll-over the debt repayment deadline as the French proposed, then a formal default would be avoided. There are of course a couple of snags. First, will bond holders extend the date of redemption and secondly will the financial market as a whole regard such appeasement as default by default? Alan Greenspan, amongst others, thinks so. And anyway, does it matter?

During the build up to this German climb down, the markets felt it very much mattered if Greece defaulted on its debt. The dreaded words Lehman and Brothers were muted as was the dreaded year 2008. Greece has already received 110bn euros with another 12bn in the pipeline and a rumour of up to a further 150bn euros in a second bailout phase. These are massive numbers for a relatively small economy and the FTSE, the German DAX and the French CAC have all been in retreat. It says it all that yields on Greek 10-year bonds reached over 17% as tension ratcheted up.

How have the Greek populace reacted to the austerity drive and the selling off of state assets? Riots and mass strikes.

Debt and more debt...

Debt and more debt – drowning in the Mediterranean stuff.

The most recent article "Greece will not default" begs an important question for the UK, namely what is the exposure to Greece and further what is the exposure to other Mediterranean states?

Like all things European, the answer is not simple. First, the UK is committed to 4.5% of international bailouts undertaken by the IMF. Specifically in relation to Greece, this amounts to about £1bn. Then there is The European Financial Stability Mechanism (EFSM). This mechanism consists of loan guarantees by all EU members which of course includes the UK albeit outside the monetary union. The UK's share is 14% and of the last chunk of the Greek loan (not actually finally agreed yet) this amounts to about 1.6bn euros. Off the hook, so to speak, relates to a third funding source called The European Financial Stability Fund (EFSF). This is a monetary union loan guarantee vehicle and so outside the scope of the UK commitment. It is however the subject of more German aid to boost the Greece economy and possibly to the tune of 211bn euros.

There are other aspects to the sea of debt. The funds described above may be thought of as Central State aid or direct taxpayer debt but UK banks have their own problems. It is believed that these banks could hold up to 13bn euros of Greek debt. Furthermore, UK banks are on the hook to other European banks themselves holding massive amounts of Greek debt (the biggest being France).

If all this is not depressing enough, we might remember that exposure to Greek debt by UK's banks is relatively small compared to say exposure to Spanish, Italian and Portuguese debt. And, if we move north to colder waters, the holding of Irish debt is in the region of 135bn euros.

Quite a headache for the UK – itself a heavily indebted state.

The day the sky fell in.

There are a number of disadvantages to being a small private investor: the worst is not being in the know. A typical 20% stop-loss will not limit damage to 20% in cases where bad news comes suddenly and unexpectedly. But, there is also one big advantage. Fleetness of foot. If a storm in gathering the small private investor can take a decision and implement it pretty much instantly and, being small, a sale will not of itself affect the market price.

A really good example is BSkyB. As soon as the scandalous news about the telephone hacking of private citizens by News Of The World rogue reporters broke, the knock-on to the then likely take-over of BSkyB by News International was obvious. The share price had risen from the £5.50 mark in the Spring of 2010 to reach about £8.50 very largely due to a muted take-out price by the 39% shareholder. If the stench of NOTW reached the nostrils of large shareholders of News Corp, then could this "sure fire" deal be in jeopardy?

As a small shareholder in BSkyB, why take the risk? On 7th July, I sold at £8.14 having bought at £5.76. Even £8.14 was not the top but due mainly to the market-makers sticking on a large spread as their insurance. The point is that the big boys couldn't move that fast and if one did, the sale order would drag the price down of its own volition.

Of course small investors will be impacted due to their indirect holding through things like unit trusts. For example, it is thought that Fidelity Special Situation with about 250,000 investors has 5.5% of its £3bn fund with BSkyB. True the price is recovering from a low of about £6.70 and the business is fundamentally a good one. Nevertheless, more recent buyers will have been stung badly and if (as is possible) News Corp has to sell their holding now the bid is aborted, the high-water mark of £8.50 may take some regaining.

M1 tailback reaches Italy.

This M1 is not the one that starts in London and crawls to Leeds. Rather, it is (mainly) currency in circulation and demand deposits. These start more or less anywhere and go more or less anywhere and a bit like the traffic on the UK's M1, it conventionally keeps on increasing and, as more lanes open up, increases further. But, something unconventional has happened en-route to Italy.

According to Simon Ward at Henderson Global Investors, "Real M1 deposits in Italy have fallen at an annual rate of 7% over the last six months, faster than during the build up to the great recession in 2008". Why does that matter? There are at least two reasons to worry:-

• A contraction in free money-flow normally presages an economic contraction.

• Italy is in the firing line of Europe's failure to agree on whether to and how to bail out Greece.

Whilst Europe's number one economic power, Germany, sits on its hands, the house of Italy (No 3) is starting to shake and the collective funds of Europe will in no way be big enough to "do a Greece" or be given the equivalent support metered to Ireland and Portugal.

The pattern of contracting money flow is not limited to Italy. France (at No 2), Austria and Belgium also have a reducing M1 and The Netherlands and Germany are in contraction mode. When this pattern occurs, one would expect central bankers to do a spot of fiscal loosening. How odd therefore that concurrently, the ECB has increased its interest rate.

Tim Congdon from International Monetary Research said, "The ECB did not see the collapse in money growth in 2008 and the great recession that followed, and they are getting it wrong again".

If you are going into mainland Europe this summer or autumn, hold off buying euros for the trip. Cheapy euro money is on the way. Perhaps.

I do not believe it!

One can hear Victor Meldrew screaming from the grave. How is it that as a direct result of the credit crisis (2008 and counting) banks that had hitherto operated with 2% core tier 1 capital, are regulated to increase this to about 10% by 2018 and then suddenly a leading guru at the Bank of England pops up with a view that weaker bank balance sheets ought to be the order of the day? I do not believe it.

Andrew Haldane, executive director of financial stability at the B of E, pointed out in a recent speech (as if anyone might forget) that President Franklin Roosevelt relaxed bank regulation in 1933 and "it worked". But, one might also feel that the US double-dip recession of 1937 comes into play?

To be fair, what Mr Haldane appeared to be advocating was that the 2.5% counter-cyclical buffer that forms part of a full 10% capital reserve could be managed without. Except of course the whole epoch of this extra safety net was to put aside in years of fat for years of lean. It is the next lean years we are supposed to be providing for, isn't it? Perhaps the signal is a psychological one, that is to say that current risk is overpriced: what do you think? Read about the economic civil war in Europe lately?

Save more and work later.

A recent article entitled "I do not believe it" commented on words of wisdom from an executive of the Bank of England. Now a colleague has also stepped up to the plate. Martin Weale, a member of the Monetary Policy Committee, propounds a view that we all need to save more and work a few more years. Here is some advice for Mr Weale, the nation knows this only too well and savings levels and silver years in the UK bear out the actual practice. The Doncaster Chamber of Commerce must have wondered what planet he had taxied from.

Trouble is the dichotomy of saying that the B of E still has the firepower of more quantitative easing at its finger tips to "provide further support to consumer spending" and such spending leading to more debt that is kind of counter to saving and working more years to pay it off. Or is it me that is up the pole? Mr Weale was apparently thinking about gilt yields at the long end of the market. I am thinking about the cash-rich large companies in the UK being encouraged to spend on large-scale capital projects of the infrastructure kind. That is what makes economic sense, not blue-sky pondering on more money printing.

Three abiding truths or stop the world I want to get off.

At the end of a week when the FTSE 100 fell 10% representing the thick end of £150billion, and this after:-

• The USA debt ceiling crisis had been compromisingly solved.

• Agreement was reached to increase the eurozone bail-out fund,

it is time for a perfectly straight drive from the pin to the first green. It is time to state the three abiding truths that seem lost in the argument, rhetoric and panic.

First, debt is debt. You can call it anything else you like and re-package it till the cows come home but if you spend more than you have, you are in debt. You could say that revenue spend debt is worse than capital spend debt. But, if the "asset" resulting from the capital spend is not easily and quickly sellable-on for more than you paid, the debt remains.

Secondly, democracy is a wonderful thing. It gives a nice warm feeling to be consensual and even altruistic. It works well if somewhat slowly in normal times when most things are well. However, none of this defeats the overarching principle that someone (that is one person) must be in charge.

Thirdly, in the world of economics, monetary and fiscal policy must work in harmony. A common currency will not work if those that make up the common herd can unilaterally decide what to do with that money.

We can now pause for breath and apply the principles to the global problems.

Every sovereign state must balance its budget, that is to say it must not spend more than its tax or asset sale revenue. Then, it sets out its long-term plan to have a surplus. It applies this surplus to its over-hanging debt, even if that takes generations. In simple terms, it stops buying from China and starts making things itself, whatever the short-term pricing cost.

The USA cannot have a so-called President who is not also the head of the political party which won most seats in its parliament. It cannot work. The eurozone body must have a head. A head that in a crisis can bang heads. There is nothing wrong with the corporate model. One chief executive, one bean-counter, one engineer and one sales & marketing supremo. Those that do not agree that body's policy are told to go and plough their own furrow.

The eurozone has a single fiscal policy. It is implemented in one of two ways. Either the deficit nations exit and return to what they used to be (which includes Italy whose debt is too big to swallow) or else there is truly shared fiscal responsibility such that Germany does much subsidising until the United States of Europe has a balance sheet it can live with and the world accepts as economically credible.

Here we go again?

All the portents say that here we go again.

Credit default swaps (CDS), which are basically insurance levels, on several big European banks have hit historic highs. CDS's on the bonds of, for example, RBS, BNP Paribas, Deutsche Bank and Intesa Sanpaolo are all flashing red. Indeed the cost of insuring RBS bonds is more now than prior to when the UK taxpayer came to the rescue in October 2008. The causal shortage of cash was always likely to override day-to-day volatility of equities and trend global markets downward. Any plus being a signal to buy quality shares for outstanding yield.

Paradoxically, big corporates are increasing profits and cash and paying back their shareholders for the record level of rights issues during 2009. The dividends of UK quoted companies this year could reach £66bn and if this happens it will represent an uplift of 16% on 2010. The alternative would have been to hoard more cash or invest in themselves. And there lies the rub. Why invest when the economic future is so uncertain? Those big banks and sovereign states have so much debt that austerity drives on consumers is about the only option left. Who would invest in idle plant?

As is only too normal in the September/October dog days, equity markets are finally getting the message that, yes really, here we go again. Yesterday, 22nd September 2011, the FTSE fell 4.7% or 246.8 points. This was the biggest drop since (wait for it), November 2008. Two other minor shivers:-

• The price of gold is falling!
• The growth in China is stalling!

China is the West in the 1970's.

High inflation and stagnant demand that is, in economic jingoism, stagflation. Thus was the Western world branded in the 1970's and thus may well be the suit that fits best the bludgeoning China.

Dr Cheng Siwei, head of Beijing's International Finance Forum is reported as saying that China is entering a "very tough period". That is, growth strangled by rampant inflation (of which wage inflation plays no small part). Chinese local authorities have built up $1.7 trillion of debt and mostly using finance vehicles. Dr Cheng thinks that defaults on this form of debt could be their version of the US subprime.

China largely avoided the 2008-2009 set-back by issuing credit on a megalithic scale. Zhu Min, the IMF's deputy chief, says that loans rose from 100% of GDP to about 200% including the dreaded off-balance sheet finance. To put this into some form of perspective, Fitch Ratings's analysis shows US credit rising by 42% of GDP in a five-year period before 2007, 45% in Japan before the Nikkei crashed in 1990 and for the Korean economy by 47% of GDP prior to their crisis in 1998.

A leading commentator and watcher of China has said that the whole world needs to lower its expectation of China. China could be thought of as a "jammed creditor" nation. Its jam is in US and other Western bond and corporate investments. To attempt a liquidation would be to self-reduce the value of this money stockpile. The commentator saying this is me. And, let's face it, who wants to be back in the 1970's?

The illusionists illusion.

Those that read my articles are likely also to follow the financial press. As such they will not have missed the juicy story of the alleged rogue trade that cost UBS £1.3bn. The official version of the happening was put out as an "unauthorised trading incident".

What may have been missed in the morass of data that was the banks' third-quarter results published on 25th October 011 was a "debt valuation adjustment". This adjustment took its authority from a widening in the bank's credit spreads, in other words, a fall in the value of its own debt. The widening was caused in part by the unauthorised trading incident. The debt valuation adjustment amounted to £1.23bn.

As a result of the adjustment adjusting the trading disaster, the Swiss bank reported a profit before tax in the quarter to September of Sfr980m. Now you see it, now you don't.

Europe is sorted then?

Yippee, the FTSE is up over 11% this month and we can all go out and spend again. It is all down to Europe, or rather the Eurozone, sorting out its money problems. Because we start and end with Greece (although tomorrow it will be Italy's turn), move one was to agree a "voluntary" agreement by private bondholders to accept a write-down of 50% on their holding of Greek debt. Whether 50% can be defined as a "credit event" seems uncertain. Such an event would cause a default of credit swaps. A default would cause further damage to rain on, for example, bank balance sheets. This takes us nicely to solution number two. A 106bn euro recapitalisation of banks will be enforced by June next year. This is our old friend "9%" which our reliable British banks already meet. The ultimate effect of move one (above) is why the means and degree of bank balance sheet strengthening is somewhat on the uncertain side.

Then we turn to Europe's bail-out fund (EFSF) that is to be leveraged "four or five times" to reach 1 trillion euros (as an aside, two different well-educated people have asked me in the last few days how many zeros there are in a trillion). To reach this magical number, a few things will be tried:-

• Risk insurance.

• Special purpose vehicles (there is a slight warning about these in my "How to read a balance sheet" section of my How to wise-up book ISBN 978-1-4466-2195-0).

• Outside investment.

On the latter possibility, the French President has already made a call to China and some very senior officials from Europe have hot-footed it over there to see what chances exist. "No charity" was one reported response (in Mandarin of course). On the other hand, Brazil and Japan are possibles and our Euorozone friends would like to get the IMF on board too although the British Chancellor will have none of this since this funder is for countries not currencies apparently.

One final spanner in the works is a German court ruling that a small group of German politicians helping to sort all this out are acting ultra vires. Still my shares are going up at last.

Public sector pension deficit plugged in one move.

A pension expert, Mr Edward Truell, whilst repeating that a study by the London School of Economics has estimated the public sector pension black hole at £1.3 trillion, has concurrently set out a plan to wipe it out.

The Treasury issues gilts to the value of the deficit and the government then uses the cash to fund infrastructure projects such as the two new gas and biomass power stations just announced for Yorkshire. It's all very simple really. The example is quoted of power plants making a 7% return on investment when the gilts has a coupon of just 2.5% so leaving a healthy margin to pay off the pension liabilities as they fall due.

There are a couple of snags of course:-

• £1.3 trillion more debt is £1.3 trillion more debt.

• Rating agencies might think that £1.3 trillion more liability on the nation's balance sheet is a bit different to the present £1.3 trillion off it; but wait, the Canadians and those clever Singaporians have already done it. Looks like the civil servants and so on will get paid after all.

Second-hand Porsches for sale, carriage from Greece is extra.

Here is an interesting statistic noted by Ian Cowie in the Daily Telegraph as researched by Professor Herakles Polemarchakis, the former head of the Greek prime minister's economic department. I just had to regurgitate it (hard to regurgitate as Polemarchakis is). There are more Porsche Cayenne Turbos in Greece than taxpayers declaring an annual income of 50k euros (£43,800). Furthermore, the modest city of Larissa, capital of the agricultural region of Thessaly, has more Porsches per head of the population than New York or London. Farming, by the way, is not buoyant in Greece and about half of a farmer's income comes from European Commission subsidies.

Now this "wow" car is made in Stuttgart that happens to be in Germany that happens to be the second largest creditor nation in the world. We are now all aware of where Greece stands in the debtor nation league table. Conclusion: export credit builds by sales to those in debt. Either debtor goes bankrupt in which case creditor bank whistles for its money or creditor unites with debtor and absorbs its debt. Either way, the Greek farmer keeps his car; unless:-

• The new national government of Greece gets tough instead of weak at the knees as well as selling off Piraeus, Peloponnisos, Corfu and a few other assets.

• It raises tax assessments on Porsche Cayenne Turbo holders and accepts the car in part-settlement.

Since this second option is new, it might just be acceptable and in which case get out your cheque book (while you still have one) and pick up a real bargain (better still get two for Christmas). After all, brand new, the car would cost £86,896 (which includes UK VAT) and it has a top speed of 173 mph and goes from zero to 62mph in 4.7 seconds. On the other hand, Greek farmers might use this tax free asset to zoom away from the mythical Greek tax man; in which case we are back where we started.

A brilliant idea.

I have just had this brilliant idea. In fact it is so brilliant I cannot conceive why no-one else seems to have thought of it.

The UK (putting up Scotland as security) buys Greece, Italy and France (not Spain since that is a favourite country of mine). It renames the whole as Stupiddebt Holdings Incorporated (translated into Mandarin) and after a period of 90 days (for memories to fade) sells the bundled package to China retaining 10% of any equity as a hedge against a debt-free future.

China absorbs its new sovereign investment into its current National Plan and puts the human assets so acquired to work. To ease monopolistic fears and as a thank you for the implemented brilliant idea, China agrees to hand Hong Kong back to the UK. Finally, the UK forms a joint trading venture with Singapore.

The new world economic league table is then:-

1. China

2. USA

3. Germany

4. UK/Singapore/Hong Kong

5. India

6. The rest.

I become non-executive chairman of UK/Singapore/Hong Kong and start work on my next brilliant idea.

Nine day trip to Germany.

Even since I started writing the credit crunch diary (captured mainly if not entirely in my book Quantitative Wheezing – ISBN 978-1-4466-6609-8) "maverick" has been the term pretty much instinctively applied to Germany. We see the maverick riding into town behind a sunset, defying all convention to shoot the baddies without proper trial and so clean up the liberal streets. He becomes sheriff provided the backlash isn't overly strong and one of his own bullets doesn't go astray and penetrate his own foot.

After unification, Germany wanted a common currency to bind a large market together and help the smaller state economies afford its luxury cars and high-value tools and machinery. What it didn't want was fiscal responsibility for those that bought the Porches on cheap credit and cash that wasn't drained by taxation. But this maverick cannot actually make the weaker brethren pull in its horns nor, as is now apparent, stop its own banks from buying the debt of those that bought its Mercedes. So when subliminal defaults occur, the bullets start to ricochet.

There is much misunderstanding about the fiscal might of Germany. German total debt is expected to rise to over 83% of its GDP before the end of December this year (011). By comparison, poor old Spain has a figure of about

61%. And the markets know it. Germany went through the routine motion of selling a relatively modest amount of its own debt this week – and failed.

What has all this to do with nine days? Nine days was the consecutive period from November 14th to November 24th that the UK FTSE dropped and primarily, thought not exclusively, due to the fiscal travails of the eurozone. That drop of 7.1% is on 100 of the biggest UK listed businesses primarily global in reach and awash with cash.

Can a maverick be downgraded? You bet it can. Can the UK have so much liquidity come next Spring to buy out Germany? Be nice to think so. The trouble with being a maverick is all those Red Indians hiding behind the rocks ready to pop up and shoot their arrows.

White knight rides forth…..

White knight rides forth, part pensioner, part Chinese man and part Local Authority Official!

We all know that "capital" is good and "revenue" is bad (usually). It makes eminent sense to spend on infrastructure projects since they provide work for skilled men and women, backroom professionals and heavy machinery. The problem in our difficult times is funding. The banks continue to be worse than useless "prove the future revenue/profit stream". It's a bit like saying to a prospective pensioner about to take out an annuity, "prove you will not live longer than 75".

Up steps white knight. And what an odd amalgam. The members of the National Association of Pension Funds (NAPF) have assets of £800bn "the pensioner". Jin Liqun is the head of China Investment Corporation and says he is keen to get involved in UK infrastructure investment "the Chinaman". Local authority funds may be used to invest in local road projects "the LA man".

So there we have it: the sources of investment finance to help kick-start things. Possibly the banks may get involved once the earnings revenue stream occurs, that is to say, when there is no risk.

Isolated from what exactly?

I beefed-up the security on my home but some in the village are saying it isolated me from the burglars.

I was once at a luncheon function at the UK House of Commons when Tarzan came swinging in from a lofty ministerial pine tree. He said a few words about Ministry of Defence procurement incompetency, gobbled a bit of food and rushed out again to meet Mrs Thatcher, who was no Jane. I mention this since that same (now Lord) Heseltine was in the early morning BBC radio car saying that we were drifting into the Atlantic, as his metaphor for isolationism from Europe, following the PM's vetoing of some form of inner constitution intended to make a fiscal union of Europe more likely.

It all means that we (the UK – though independent Scotland is balking) are feared to be isolating ourselves from:-

• 400bn euros needing to be rolled over by Italy in 2012 and some 150bn by Spain where bond yields stand currently at 6.8% and 5.8% respectively.

• A bath full of water where Greece, as the plug, is about to be pulled.

• An erosive threat to our tax take from financial services amounting to 11.2% of total tax take (source – report by PwC).

• A sticky if not moribund bond market in the face of yields on UK and USA gilts that have hardly ever been lower.

• The euro as an instrument of monetary union has been an unmitigated disaster (try buying a coffee in Paris).

• New rules being avoided by the UK are not new, something called the Growth & Stability Pact was within the Maastricht Treaty. Neither growth nor stability occurred because rules were broken and were un-policed. More rules will go the same way.

• Etc, etc, etc.

When Germany sells cars and machinery paid for only by debt, only German assumption of that debt will solve the problem. Just like the burglar out there, best stay isolated.

No chance of a second Credit Crunch.

What makes my book Quantitative Wheezing (ISBN 978-1-4466-6609-8) unique is that it catalogues the credit crunch crisis of 2008-2010 and such a crisis of credit availability cannot recur, at any rate in the UK. How come, you might reasonably ask.

The Bank of England is offering access to a new supply of emergency sterling funding. This new source of credit will be called The Extended Collateral Term Repo (ECTR). It is a contingency plan under which the B of E will give lenders access to month-long sterling loans if current "exceptional stresses" on global financial markets caused by the eurozone's difficulties spread to the UK's interbank lending market (see my article "Isolation from what exactly").

Before the collective sigh of relief, it is worth mentioning that the UK has £140bn of debt maturing in 2012. Still, ECTR sounds grand enough to perform the trick.

Zombie.

The first definition in The Chambers Dictionary 11th Edition (there are plenty of other explanations) is "A corpse reanimated by sorcery".

Or, in current banking parlance, a bank which relies on central funding to survive. If banks in the newly further-enhance bureaucratized Europe make excessive use of three-year long-term refinancing operations (LTRO), they will become addicted to the ECB. This addiction thus turns the banks into zombies. To recognise a zombie is to get out of its way pronto. That is why lenders to European banks are selling trillions of euro assets to reduce their exposure.

New figures released by the Bank of England show that in the three months to the end of September 011, British banks reduced their exposure to French banks by £19bn (10%) and by about £13bn to Italian and Spanish banks. Conversely, exposure to German assets rose by £26bn. Other big increases went the Dutch and American way.

Coincidentally, as I was withdrawing from a chat with a Greek gentleman in the sauna yesterday and who was sweating over a decision whether to return to his homeland or stay in his now preferred home of England, I heard myself saying as I left the humid atmosphere "As usual Britain will end up going its own way".

We vetoed a fiscal pact that within seven days is falling apart at the seams (if it was ever stitched that is). The fiscal compact commits countries to keeping their primary deficits below 0.5% of GDP and debt levels to below 60% of GDP. Not a cat in hells chance. Not even a dead cat bounce chance.

489 followed by nine euro noughts = 523.

Half a trillion is slightly easier to get ones head around and 523 is the number of banks which rushed to get at this huge number of euros put up for grabs by the European Central Bank (ECB) at a coupon of 1%. The rush to the December sales is not surprising given that it is estimated that European banks will have to repay 600bn euros during 2012 and the wholesale markets are, in the main, frozen.

This largest-ever scale of quantitative easing goes into the vaults of those banks in return for illiquid assets. Irrespective of the real security or otherwise of this collateral, what matters is that future wholesale money market debt will stand subordinate to this ECB debt and therefore future calls on the normal wholesale funding will necessarily be more expensive than otherwise would be the case. Certainly more expensive that 1%.

What will happen to the new funds? Theories range over:-

• Lent to blue-chip corporate borrowers at a considerable mark-up.

• Lent out to undercut banks not taking the cheap money.

• Buy sovereign debt from the likes of Greece and Portugal but it is this sort of debt that has been swapped with the ECB anyway.

Are we any nearer to solving the European economic problem? Probably not.

World stock market indexes 2011.

In a word – disaster: a bad dream for those with investments and on fixed incomes. I have gathered some statistics and grouped sovereign states into five to see if any sense can be made of the year as it fell apart all over again. This analysis starts with Europe (see my article "Zombie") and ends with the New World economy. Each statistic is the percentage change from 1st January 011 to 23rd December 011 on each named index of stocks. The performance is in descending order.

Europe.

Ireland ISEQ -1.0

UK FTSE 100` -7.0

Germany DAX -17.0

Spain Micex -18.0

France CAC40 -22.0

Portugal PSI -23.0

Italy MIB -25.0

Greece ASE20 -62.0

Emerging economies.

Brazil Bovespa -17.0

Russia Micex -18.0

China Shangai Composite -22.0

India Sensex -23.0

Established Asia.

Japan Nikkei -18.0

Hong Kong Hang Seng -21.0

African Spring.

Tunisia TUSISE -8.0

Egypt EGX30 -50.0

New World.

USA Dow Jones +5.0

USA S&P 500 -0.2.

If we disregard Ireland since just three companies make up about half of the index and at the other end of the scale, the USA Dow lists only 30 businesses, albeit the biggest ones, we see a spread of no real change in America to the UK heavyweights having the least fall of all the main stock market indices. Mainland Europe has been a mass of red ink with Greece earning the wooden spoon with India having the largest set-back of the erstwhile new thrusters. Perhaps as surprising as any decline has been that of Japan and Hong Kong.

The historical lesson for the wealth managers and the diversified portfolio holders is stay faithful to the good old "new world" and loyal to the FTSE with its global spread of businesses. One final observation: the greenback and the pound have become, once again, safe havens for cash. 2011, the year of dreadful surprise.

An ill-wind blows Jag eastwards.

It's an ill-wind that blows no good. The ill-wind that blew a gale from the West weakened sterling as an international currency. And that is where the good bit comes in. A relatively weak pound, in contrast to the mighty US dollar that appreciated during 2011 by some 9%, is good for exports. That, in turn, is where the Jag comes in.

Jaguar Land Rover (JLR) reported a profit of £1.1bn in 2011 and it was the export market that did it. Grouped alongside the likes of Toyota, Nissan and BMW (the again all-conquering Mini), JLR provided an astonishing statistic, namely that for November 2011, 88% of all cars made in Britain were exported. All together it is expected that about 1.1 million cars will leave UK shores in 2011 making that performance close to the record set in 2007, that is, before the ill-wind wafted in from the US sub-prime crisis.

A real feel-good factor from the motor manufacturing boost to the UK economy is that £4bn of new investment will have been made before the year is out and there are to be new engine plants and many new jobs created. The car industry accounts for some 10% of Britain's total export value and employs at least 700,000 people.

Aside from statistics, the real and lasting joy about today's British built cars is that they are excellently engineered, superbly styled across the market segments and, best of all, appreciated by the expanding Eastern markets as quality at its British finest.

As the year ends, we can put aside the issue of who ultimately owns the new British marques and how we got here. The fact is a success story is worth a bit of tub-thumping.

Playing this crazy monetary game.

In my article "489 followed by 9 euro noughts ....", three possibilities were propounded as to what the 532 banks would do with this massive call on ECB reserves. None was correct – at least except to a tiny degree. Statistics have shown that as much as 95% of the funds drawn down were (wait for it) deposited back with the central bank. Can you believe it?

Playing the monetary game is the latest craze in town. Those who have read my piece on Quantitative Easing will know that the Bank of England does not physically print money, rather it credits the account of the seller's bank held by itself. A startling result of the QE programme is that the B of E now holds circa 20% of all UK gilts on issue. So, albeit indirectly via the "seller" of securities, the central bank of the UK is the buyer of UK debt! What this amounts to is that the money pumped into the economy is being used to buy issued debt to support that same economy.

Students of accountancy will know what a "contra" entry is. A debit can be used to wipe out the same amount of credit to regain neutral. Just suppose the B of E was nationalised by the UK government and just suppose the ECB was nationalised by the European monetary union. Can you work out where the new money will be?

Part 4

Nevertheless - smile again.

The eurozone monetary and fiscal woes continue with in particular the holders of Greek debt losing at least half their locks and even contributing to the all-powerful Deutsche Bank sustaining a loss in the last quarter. Middle-Eastern non-democratic tension and violence continues unabated, allegations of Russian election fraud excite frozen protestations in Moscow and Chinese peasants revolt.

Nevertheless, we can smile again. This is because the UK's service sector, which accounts for about three-quarters of all annual income, is growing and actually quite steeply. What! Who says so? PMI, that's who. The Purchasing Managers' Index rose to a remarkable "56" in January 012 (a ten-month high) where any notch above 50 means expansion. It is of course all to do with the private sector and, to be fair, the public sector hasn't actually shrunk that much notwithstanding all the political tub-thumping. But aside from services, both manufacturing and construction developed in January.

Furthermore, the Bank of England clearly cares more about getting growth back into the UK economy than risking higher inflation and to a degree that rumours of more quantitative easing abound. Most money is on a further

£50bn of the stuff to bring the total to date to £325bn. So smile we are in for a good year.

Our old friend, the FTSE, is on side too. It reached 5,901 at close of business yesterday. Finally let's recall that the US economy is by some way still the largest in the world and, guess what, unemployment dropped to 8.3% in January and so down from the high of last August of 9.1%.

All in all, time to smile again.

Call for new by-pass to ease annuity woes.

Given the almost certainty that a further quantitative easing programmes will be announced later this week, maybe it's time the motivation theory is challenged. The idea is that the first £275bn was pumped into the UK economy to, inter-alia, allow financial institutions to release funds to lend to businesses. But, according to research by the accountants Ernst & Young, bank lending is set to fall for the first time in three years. Those hardest hit are expected to be:-

• SME's.

• Commercial real estate funders and,

• Personal customers falling outside standard credit terms.

A clarion call can be made. Lend the next £50bn or so directly to small businesses. Such a bank by-pass would benefit that strata of the community who used to have, and could still have, the power to spend. This is because a direct consequence of the B of E's gilt purchases (the QE programme) is to reduce the yield from the gilt market. This in turn lowers the annuity rate on the pension pot sold to the insurance company or whoever. Not only that, the size of a business's pension liability increases proportionately.

What is needed is a new by-pass. What is needed is real help for SME's. Not the sham of open doors where a bank is quoting an overdraft rate of 7.4% above base and a £2k set-up fee – oh, and a personal guarantee on top. Some risk is that.

Fool's gold.

Warren Buffett, writing in a forthcoming shareholder letter published by Fortune magazine (Harry Wallop in the Daily Telegraph) produced some very interesting "anti-gold as an investment" figures.

At current prices – about $1,717 an ounce – the world's total supply at 170,000 tonnes is worth $9.6 trillion. With that sum one could buy all of America's farmland or 16 Exxon Mobils and still have $1 trillion left over. The former has an annual return of $200bn and the latter $640bn. Gold bullion has no yield.

Meantime, Coutts, the bank, has predicted that gold prices will hit new highs in 2012.

Who are you backing?

Barclays' fiddle-stick accounting.

Not for the first time a leading bank has played around with the movement in the value (as at a specific date) of its own debt. In the case of Barclays we are dealing with the small matter of £2.7bn. Under the old UK GAAP rules, this "credit" would have been excluded from the profit before tax figure. But, Barclays conformed to the (highly criticised) International Financial Reporting Standards (IFRS) and so included the book gain. Also, under GAAP "impairment charges" would of course be deducted before striking profit simply since this charge is basically depreciation by any other name.

So, dear old Barclays, sensitive as ever to criticism, decided to publish a separate pre-tax profit that excludes the controversial debt value gain. Good. Except not quite because this separate statement also excludes the impairment figure (£2.8bn) derived from selling Black Rock and also the small matter of £597m charge arising from the PPI mis-selling scandal. Clever isn't it? Now you see it, now you don't.

Does it matter? Well, the revised profit is £5.6bn. Under GAAP rules, it would be £2.9bn. Oh, and separately, Pensions & Investment Research Consultants (PIRC) noticed that Barclays has spread the accounting cost of its bonus payments over three years. The deferral means that £2bn in excluded from the P&L account this year.

Barclays confirmed its compliance with accounting standards.

Subtle transfer of wealth.

Of course it wasn't done for this reason: it was done to stimulate the economy.

Nevertheless, the Bank of England's decision last week to pump another £50bn of funds using the Quantitative Easing programme and to make £325bn in total has the by-product of easing those in debt at the expense of those wanting safe (ish) income from savings.

Demand for gilts raises the capital value and consequentially lowers the return or yield. Not good, again, for savers and for those minded to purchase annuities for their retirement income. But, very good for borrowers who can now have a clear long-term vision of loan and mortgage rates not inflating. Since the income enjoyed by the silver-tops was spent fairly freely on holidays and grandchildren and various comfort items, taking away their bread will need some compensation from more money sloshing around.

It's quite a tricky equation really not least because the bank of mum and dad and granny and granddad plays a major part in getting those first-time buyers started on the property ladder, yet when the old codger income dries up so also does that "stimulus" kick.

The jury is out but anyway the rating agency Fitch thinks the UK is in a better position than Germany which cannot print its own dosh. And yet again, creating cash out of thin air does seem a touch wrong especially to an old codger generation that was brought up to think that money had to be earned.

Ending with Germany, some commentators think we do not after all have a Greece crisis. It is a German one.

Be cheered by the US of A.

Given the bombardment of a plethora of economic data and not least all the gloomy stuff, it is worth using a perspective on the scale of the wealth power of America. The USA is by far the greatest single generator of GDP in the world. It is way ahead of the now number two China who may catch up in absolute terms in 20 years time and may not and expressed per capita, arguably never will.

Set in this context, it is very significant that the Dow Jones Industrial Average hit 13,005 shortly before lunchtime on 21st February 2012, a figure last achieved in May 2008. The agreement on the bailout for Greece was an obvious trigger but more likely is the gathering hope that America is poised in 2012 to recover its economic verve significantly.

The iconic New York based Macy's has just reported profits well above those expected and the clever Dow in anticipation of the fun to come is already up 5% this calendar year.

Maybe the flash-point daily news spells out the European gloom but folks in Florence, Paris, Brussels, Milan and Barcelona are partying the nights away in American-based Hard Rock Café outlets.

Quantitative easing – front and now back door.

I am willing to bet that you thought, as I did, that the emergency programme set up by the European Central Bank (ECB) and called "the long-term refinancing operation" LTRO was to ward off an impending collapse of mainland Europe's financial system. That is to say, providing liquidity to the eurozone sovereign states. In so far as most of the one trillion euros are concerned it was, indeed, about half of the notes were picked up by Italian and Spanish institutions. The surprise package comes in an admission that British banks namely Lloyds, Barclays, RBS and HSBC have also dipped in to secure loans at the amazingly advantageous rate of 1%.

The headline figure of borrowings by British banks from the ECB is £22bn this week when the LTRO presented a second tranche of loans to add to whatever was taken up in November 011 when the initial opportunity arose. The point at issue to us non-bankers is what will happen to these new pennies? It is reported that analysts at Morgan Stanley think that the mainland Europeans will use the money to buy their own Government's bonds. If so, this will mirror the £325bn of quantitative easing activated by the Bank of England once the latest round is completed about May time. In other words, the

UK pumped in liquidity by a direct route, let's call it by the front door, whilst our European colleagues used the back door.

Let us suppose next that these cheap loans are used (in the UK or elsewhere) to buy back the recipient bank's own bonds. That will be a nice little earner – again. Of course, such profit will be ring-fenced from any remuneration pot, at any rate according to Barclays. Then again, read my earlier articles on Barclays accounting methodology.

Dust off the trumpet.

Woe to ye misery mongers.

History dictates that the best investment opportunities are nascent when the future as purveyed by the pundit experts plunges the depths of despair . With a bellyful of Eurozone frazzle, it is time to move on.

The FTSE hit 5,965, a 2012 high, at the end of last week and according to research by Citigroup the next ten years could see a doubling in its overall value, so jump aboard the ETF and index tracker train now. According to the research findings, corporate earnings will increase by 6% p.a. and dividends by 4%. Coupled with hoards of cash, the scene is set for a surge in merger & acquisition activity and share buy-backs.

The research note emphasises the fact that the big UK companies are truly international and not least in the commodity sector. Strong balance sheets lead to fire power and cheaper debt. This means that money "eventually has to be spent".

I am with Citigroup. In 4p rise time, my Taylor Wimpey shares break even.

The $700bn "no profit" call.

On 13th November 2008 I wrote an article challenging the logic of the TARP $700bn bail out fund of the US economy. Notwithstanding that the original target for the bail out was changed in favour of investing in the banks and non-financial companies such as the auto industry, I stuck to my view that bundling packages of rubbish into one big pile of rubbish, did not remove or cleanse that rubbish.

A report from the watchdog of the TARP programme now believes that the eventual loss to US taxpayers will be $60bn (8.5%). Taxpayers are still owed $119bn and the majority of that is still tied up in the rescue of insurer AIG (which, by winding up the European arm, PriceWaterhouseCoopers still makes a few bob from) and General Motors and Ally Financial.

The report into the progress of TARP goes on to say that the programme, "may have prevented the immediate collapse of our financial and auto manufacturing industries, but a significant legacy of TARP is increased moral hazard and potentially disastrous consequences associated with institutions deemed too big to fail".

What is the lesson some three-and-a-half years on? Things gone wrong have to fail. It is the only worthwhile, albeit painful, lesson. Why not apply that lesson to the Eurozone? Lance it now or the long lingering death awaits.

Spanish manana.

If only Spain's tomorrow could be like Spain's yesterday, then Spain's today would not be so horrible.

The Spanish housing bust is the bust of all busts. In 2007, Spanish builders created 750,000 new (potential) homes. The annual market is estimated at 250,000 houses. How did this come about? How was it financed? The answer is that for the past ten years or so real rates of interest were around minus 2%. Cheap money from Northern Europe allowed Spain to post a 3% GDP surplus in that year whilst public debt fell to 42%. Drunk on white vino and drunk on credit: something had to give.

Once the ECB tightened its monetary policy, Spain's measure of real M1 (the most liquid measure of money supply) fell at the rate of 8% in the second half of 2011 thus making a crash into severe recession absolutely certain. 24.4% of work-able Spaniards are idle.

The Bankia has just received a 23bn euro bail out following hard on the heels of a 4bn euro one and so creating a nationalised bank previously created from seven regional "savings" banks. This savings monolith has a black hole of 30bn euros of bad debts ex property developers. All told, the Centre for European Policy Studies believes that the whole of the Spanish banking system needs to write off 270bn euros of bad loans.

The latest bit of doom news is that regions have window-dressed their accounts by failing to pay suppliers some 17bn euros. For example, Valencia is 765 days late on bills. Because of the eurozone, Spain cannot:-

• Devalue its currency.

• Print money.

• Trigger a lender of last resort.

It can only weep. But weeping lasts only so long. The Latin Bloc is stirring.

Turn again Merkel, Lord Mayor(ess) of Berlin.

That the golden dawn of a 100bn euro bail out of Spanish banks by the EU (forget the actual institution – present or future – it's too confusing and makes no difference anyway unless of course you are a Spanish bondholder) lasted until just coffee time that morning, was surely the turning point for Germany. The so-called European Redemption Pact (ERP) or, in accounting parlance, a sinking-fund was dismissed summarily last November by Mrs Merkel as "totally impossible". But that was before two very important things happened.

First, German opposition Greens and Social Democrats backed such a plan and the Chancellor needed their votes for a two-thirds majority to ratify the EU Fiscal Treaty. Secondly, heavy pressure arrived at Berlin's door from the US, China, the UK and Southern Europe to change tack before it was too late to avoid a global melt-down.

Proof: yields on 10-year Spanish debt reached a dangerous 6.8% yesterday and thus wafted away any remaining bail-out euphoria. A disease is one thing. Its contagious affect quite another. As Andrew Roberts of RBS put it "I feel very sorry for Italy. They have done the hard work over the years and have a cyclically-adjusted surplus". Knock-on in a common market is self-fulfilling. Italy had to pay 3.97% to raise its latest debt compared with 2.34% only last month.

What ERP actually consists of is highly technical but it is the opposite of fiscal union since each country would be responsible for its own share of the total debt in the sinking fund and have to pledge collateral security such as gold reserves and equal to 20% of their debt in the whole fund.

The ERP idea was drafted by Germany's Council of Economic Experts, colloquially known as the five wise men. Though not as wise as the inventor; one Alexander Hamilton in 1790!

Alone again, naturally.

The UK Chancellor George Osborne gave his Mansion House speech last night in words echoing the spirit of Dunkirk 1940. He was emphasising that the UK is not powerless in facing the eurozone debt crisis. We can bring new weaponry forward to face the fiscal and monetary enemy and reinforce the now very tired troops of the quantitative easing and low interest rate battalions.

The Bank of England is to make available £140bn of emergency credit (43% of the QE programme to date) with the objective of helping banks to re-ignite the domestic mortgage and small company loan market. It will not have escaped the attention of all those whose house loans have reached their two-year expiry date that rates have gone up substantially in the interim. A secondary objective is to barricade British banks from the anticipated fall-out from the eurozone crisis since this credit line will substitute for international finance.

How will the scheme work? In return for the money lent, banks will swap assets such as mortgage books. Note that with the QE programme, the B of E bought government bonds and so put liquidity in the market in a sort of second-hand way. This new battle tactic is more direct.

History shows what happened post 1940. Can we stand alone and win again?

More dosh: no dice.

It crept in with the quietest of whimpers; the BBC gave it about seventh billing in its evening news bulletin. It might only be 15% of what had gone on before but still, £50bn is an awful lot of money. The Bank of England's monetary policy committee decided yesterday to quantitatively ease a bit more. The continued orthodoxy of buying gilts by the UK central bank is disheartening and would be boring where things not so serious. Why should it work when there is little evidence that the prior £325bn did? Does the bank really want to hold 40% of its own Government's debt?

Coincidentally on the same day, the ECB and China tried a different tack in an effort to stimulate the global economy. Both cut interest rates and the euro fell to a three-and-a-half year low against sterling. And, having just paid 6 euros for a 330ml goblet of beer in France, how that is needed!

In the UK, what else is happening to kick-start things out of the double-dip recession? Well, there is a new "funding for lending" scheme and eight UK city councils have been given the go-ahead to borrow against future revenue to spend on capital projects. But, all in all and down at street level, it's the price of petrol and diesel, stupid! But those at the top are not at street level and do not see the knock-on from filling a tank at £100 a time (it's no cheaper in France either). But like the LIBOR and PIP insurance and derivative selling before it, any corrective/punitive action will be too little too late.

What a fine mess. More dosh? No dice mate.

Alice in suckerland.

At the risk of agreeing with the Red Queen, sentence first verdict afterwards, it always seemed logical to think that those in high places being highly educated and highly paid, would be respected. No so any more.

LIBOR (Lie is black or red) manipulation by low-balling was hinted at by the NY Fed. back in the now infamous 2008 year when the financial world was rocking. But the Bank of England didn't cotton on, one of the sheriff's deputies didn't mark the card of the head of Barclays (referred to times many in these articles as Maverick) on instruction from high sources in Whitehall and that head of Barclays (off with his head said the Red Queen) didn't specifically order his operations chief to rig the rate submitted. Yet that head of operations said it all happened. Curiouser and curiouser.

Profit from thyself – impossible.

All my lifelong training and experience says that making profit from oneself is impossible. "Profit" by definition is added value at the expense of another party. Unless maybe we think of a non-accounting definition of profit such as Shakespeare's to make progress, to improve. Even then, there is surely some other party involved, somebody or something that has "given" so you could "take".

So, it is fascinating to learn that moving funds from one arm of government to another arm could make the UK £30bn by next year. How come? According to Michael Saunders, UK economist at Citi (article by Philip Aldrick – DT 15th August 2012), the QE programme that we are all now so familiar with loaded the Bank of England with gilts that themselves earn interest from our own treasury. The critical point being that the "purchase" cost nothing since the money used came out of thin air.

The article referred to is really about how the "profit" from the QE programme could be used, that is, should we delay deficit reduction or perhaps have a tax giveaway. But the fact is, there is nothing to use because the profit is artificial. It is a monetary smoke and mirrors trick. There is a cost and accounting principles are not flawed. If £30bn "profit" is made, then £30bn cost will arise. The cost will be in the loss

198

of purchasing power of future money (inflation) including the real worth of what is owned to creditors (the owners of debt). Mr Saunders worries about the calling into question of the B of E's credibility if UK's fiscal options were to depend on monetary policy. No need to worry about that: credibility on calling inflation was shot to ribbons by the figures out yesterday. The "cost" side of the so-called QE profit is already revealing itself.

PS. The US Federal Reserve gives its earnings from gilts obtained by money printing back to the US Treasury account each week. Interest out – same interest in. Wither no profit. Case proved.

China v Japan – small bits of land – huge consequence.

Two years ago and in Kuala Lumpur a friend of mine mentioned the smouldering tension that was the Senkaku/Diaoyu islands in the East China Sea. Like, I suspect, most Westerners it was news to me. It isn't any more, nor to you.

Cutting to the chase, a gentleman named Jin Baisong of the Chinese Academy of International Trade (part of the commerce ministry) has written a piece in China Daily advocating the "security exception" rule under the WTO to punish Japan over its decision to nationalise the disputed small bits of land. The crucial point is that China is Japan's biggest creditor holding some £141bn of its bonds and dumping all of some of these assets could well bring Japan's already tricky fiscal position to one of crisis.

Compounding such a threat, the Hong Kong Economic Journal has reported that China is drawing up plans to cut off the supply to Japan of rare earth metals (the accumulated near-monopoly of supply by China has been commented on before in these articles) used in the hi-tech industries of Japan. Then there is Fitch Ratings downgrade threats on Japanese exporters to China if tensions are not eased. For example, Nissan sends 26% of its cars to China and Honda 20%. Mr Jin went further saying that

China can sacrifice its "low-value-added" exports to Japan at a small cost.

Economic warfare is one thing: social attacks quite another. Anti-Japanese protests have spread to 85 cities across China and forced Japanese companies to close their factory gates.

We all know about the historical enmity: we also know about what Chinese nationalistic uprising can lead to. One feels a cold shudder.

Corporation tax, and how to avoid it.

Whilst sipping my Americano this morning, this interesting snippet popped up (Helia Ebrahimi, DT).

In the latest accounts Costa Coffee as owned by Whitbread paid corporation tax of £15m or 30.5% of its profits derived from £377m sales. Starbucks with sales of £398m paid nothing in corporation tax, indeed has a £8.9m tax credit brought forward. Is the disparity down to inefficiency by the American megalith with a market capitalisation of $40bn? Possibly. But there was the matter of a 6% royalty paid by the wholly owned UK subsidiary to its US parent (note: not a franchise) and no doubt buried within an "administrative expenses" heading of £107.2m (26.9% of turnover).

There must be an awful lot of people toiling behind that coffee counter. There might be an awful lot to challenge by HMR&C.

The new Bond film.

Definition of film, "a coating of a sensitive substance".

If there is to be a new credit bubble, it is likely to arise from a resurgent corporate bond market. Thus we have a new bond film.

If one is a safe investor, and try getting anything above 2.5% gross of tax at the moment, then the current flurry of corporate bond issues is very tempting, maybe overwhelmingly so. Statistics show that last month alone, UK companies raised £17.3bn of debt and this was more than twice the figure for the corresponding September 011. Research by Thompson Reuters shows that £1.4bn of debt raised in September 012 was in junk bonds (previous year – nil). Also, September witnessed a large surge in US dollar denominated debt.

What is happening and does it matter? Dozens of private equity-backed companies are queuing to jump on a "better return" bandwagon and these range from the RAC through Formula 1 to Iglo. In so far as equity is swapped for debt in reasonable amounts to pay investors, well and good. But, history tells us to be careful not to overburden corporates with leverage especially as it can be argued that once the financial world pulls itself together, interest rates can go only one way and that is up. A related issue is that according to Moody's £111bn of junk classified corporate debt is due for repayment over the next two years and half of this lies with just 27 companies.

I note that my own holding of corporate fixed income is 18% of the investment portfolio. Seems about right.

Of nuclear pickle.

Three articles ago was a short piece called "China v Japan …." It is worth a re-read since things are getting worse with naval and other "military training" now taking place off-shore the Islands in question. It is hard to find sympathy for Japan although presumably we in the UK should since apparently the USA is now a strong ally. Shudder again.

What is really odd is that Japan (through Hitachi) has bought, and from two German companies, a stake in the UK's nuclear future notwithstanding the recent disaster in Japan. Even more perverse is that a Japanese company has delivered an even greater blow to UK pride by buying Branston Pickle from Premier Foods. How will the Japanese economy shadow the enterprise of its private companies? The answer of course is that it will ease itself forward yet again.

The Bank of Japan has announced it is to spend £86bn (11 trillion yen) – a further 13.75% on the total "eased" so far – on buying more government and corporate bonds and commercial paper. It will also provide new loans to banks. Japan's trade figures for September 2012 were the worst for more than 30 years which in no small part takes us back to where we started, namely the trade war with China.

Once the US stops looking inward to its new President, it must with some urgency cast an eye Westward over the Pacific.

Basel 111 and the back burner.

The Basel 111 rules which were agreed two years ago and have received regulatory approval by the UK, USA and European authorities, require banks to hold loss-absorbing capital equivalent to 7% of the size of their individual risk-weighted assets. For the biggest banks this % is increased to 9.5. The over-arching purpose of Basel 111 is to ensure that governments never again have to bail out these big lenders (the "too big to fail" scenario). The deadline set is 1st January 2013: there is however a snag.

Appearing as long ago as 1991 in The Collins English Dictionary, the back burner long since had anything to do with slow cooking. Rather is means a delaying tactic or equally likely a kill-off.

If one takes the view that holding this degree of frozen capital dissuades banks from lending to the needy in these times of economic crisis, then one might think it prudent to need more time to understand and implement. If consequently (say) the UK-based banks implement Basel 111 on time whilst (say) the USA ones do not, then it is not difficult to imagine that New York will score against its London rival as the leading financial centre.

The US Treasury has said that American banks will not be ready.

Are back burners selling rapidly in London?

Magic roundabout.

This short article has the potential to be misleading in that you might think something has happened when in fact it hasn't. The illusion works like this :-

• The Bank of England, an organ of the state, plucks £375bn out of thin air.

• It uses this electronic credit to actually purchase UK Treasury debt: the Treasury being another organ of the same state.

• Because the quantum of purchases is great, the act of purchasing causes the market price of the gilt-edged securities in question to rise whilst the coupon of the bond stays at the issue price.

• A combination of the Bank's £375bn state asset's increase in capital value and the yield it produced (paid by the Treasury of course), produces a "profit".

• £35bn of this profit is to be taken by the Treasury from the Bank of England.

The £35bn of profit taken by the Treasury will be used to reduce the current budget deficit, the Government's accumulate debt (£1.159 trillion this year or 72% of GDP) and obviously the sum paid in debt interest since this pile of debt is consequently reduced.

But, wait a minute. One organ of the state has bought debt from another organ of the state and received interest on that debt from the first party, to now pay it back with book capital appreciation. Magic.

Apparently the independent Office of Budget Responsibility will soon assess the "long-term cost" of the "profit" and some other body is thinking about the accounting entries. Some wag referred to smoke and mirrors. I fail to see the smoke but the mirrors are there alright.

Mr Abe versus his own bank.

Over the past four years I have written many articles on the state of Japan which, lest we forget, is still the world's third largest economy. Japan's Liberal Democratic Party (LDP), as headed by Mr Shinzo Abe, has just won a two-thirds "super-majority" landslide victory at the polls. So what one might well ask. So a seismic economic change is under way, or so leading Japan-watchers say. Professor Richard Werner of Southampton University is a strong critic of the Bank of Japan and is quoted as saying " …. tight-money/loose fiscal mix has pushed (Japan's) public debt to 240% of GDP. The bank should have stopped the rot immediately by flooding the money supply to kick-start lending. It has taken 20 years and the Fed's Ben Bernanke to show them how to do it". This is where Mr Abe comes in.

The Japan LDP fought the election on a stimulus ticket and only too aware of the anti-inflation policies of the central bank, backed its expansionary vision with a direct threat to bring in a new law to force its will on the bank should it prove necessary. Commentators see a big change in Japan heralding a fresh reflation cycle on a global scale and quote improved numbers from the US as underpinning this view.

Mr Abe intends to charge an economic council to shift dramatically both fiscal and monetary strategy and has set this council a 3% growth target. This may not sound much but compared to nil growth over the past 15 years, it is actually profound in its reach. Furthermore, things are already happening. The yen is depreciating against the US dollar, the Nikkei is up 10% and there is to be a blitz of foreign bond purchases on the Swiss model. What does it all mean? A whirlwind of quantitative easing on a world scale, that's what. But history teaches us that Japan is not the US nor is it the UK. Mr Abe can expect a fight with his own bank. Japanese people hope he can win.

A watered-down Basel 111.

A key part of the Basel 111 reform package agreed by regulators across the world and designed to make banks more secure and able to act resolutely in the event of financial crisis, is know as LCR (liquidity coverage ratio). No doubt as a nod to low economic growth globally, the timing agreed previously for reaching the ratio, has been extended.

The Basel Committee on Banking Supervision has announced that banks affected need only have 60% of the necessary short-term funding in place by 2016 and have until 2019 to implement fully. In addition, the Committee has said that the lenders would be able to run down their pool of liquid assets below the minimum threshold "during periods of stress".

It should be added perhaps that there is much discontent with how international accounting standards allow the portrayal of banking performance with insufficient weight placed on doubtful debts as distinct from actual bad debts.

The watered-down agreement had an immediate affect on banking share prices around the world. The STOXX Europe 600 Bank index hit a 17-month high on 7th January 013. Unbelievably, my Lloyds Group holding is now less that 50% down!

A load of New Year bull.

I am indebted to a piece in the Daily Telegraph for the statistics contained in this short article and in turn their reliance on figures from EPFR Global.

After, for the most part, a horrible 2012 on the main stock markets, the compromise last-minute deal on the US so-called fiscal cliff and timed propitiously for the first day of 2013 heralded a global bull run. World-wide investors punted £13.6bn into equities in the week ending 9th January, the second highest inflow since 2000.

Domestically, the FTSE 100 has risen to 6,121 being its highest level since May 2008. The UK's more representative FTSE 250 also scaled a new high to 12,798. There has to be hope (but watch out for the "US debt ceiling" to replace the fiscal cliff) that a sustained equity rally has set in with a two-fold gain from cash leaving bonds such that bond yields rise to give a higher return for annuities.

A FTSE 250 member that, as much as any other single share, epitomises the maelstrom of a share price since 2008 is the big builder Taylor Wimpey. Trading at around 135p in early 2008, a low of less than 10p occurred by early 2009 followed by a roller-coaster till it reached around 40p by mid 2012. The new year 2013 saw it reach 74p (admittedly ahead of pending results). The key and more than academic point (for me) is, can the share get back to its 2008 level? To do so, it must climb by a further 82%, and my new Mercedes will be on order.

Miss flighty footsie flirts het Mr Bond.

Having desisted from jumping off Manhattan Bridge, American Markets sent a coded message to its like kind. The smart boys with their bags of cash and bundles of bonds cracked the code with ease and off flew Miss Equity 2013.

How ironic that Mr Medvedev could be the one to keep the party going?

Notwithstanding the economic eschewers and the Davos doomsters, the fact is markets look ahead and the cold damp winter is turning to spring: snowdrops are out. With oodles of cash and gold back in fashion, why shouldn't we raise a glass?

The UK FTSE 100 has passed 6,300 for the first time since prior Lehman and actually since May 2008 (at time of writing 6,345). With a plus of 6.7% since January 1st, this is the strongest start of any year since 1989.

We are aware of China's stockpile of foreign reserves and its increasing appetite for gold and hard assets but Russia may have slipped slightly under the radar. With the world's third largest holding of foreign reserves – estimated at about $500bn – Russian premier Dmitry Medvedev talking to the German daily Handelsblatt is reported as saying "We now have a different mission: 42% of our reserves are euros, so we could get rid of them by investing in equities". Since the Russian premier is known to be highly critical of the present state of economic Europe "miserable condition", there seems little logical reason why Russian reserves should not flirt with Miss UK FTSE 100. Due largely to our old friend QE, bond prices are too high, so most likely a het to that alternative.

The point is, will UK equity markets continue to rise? Looking at new data from the US & China and the external view of Europe as expressed in Russia, the answer could well be yes. And, of course, it is not academic. Our share portfolios and our pension pots are screaming "yes, yes, do it to me again"

Spain's head is out of the water.

So declared Mariano Rajoy, the Spanish prime minister during his state-of-the-nation address to the parliament in Madrid; the streets of which were once again filled with disgruntled Spaniards last weekend. Let's hope he is right. The waters around Spain and its islands can be choppy this time of year and I am off to Lanzarote soon.

The figures underlying the premier's statement do give substance to the spirit of the "getting better" rhetoric. The budget deficit has improved to less than 7% for 2012. The comparative for 2011 was 9.4%. Consequently, Spain's borrowing costs have reduced. The yield on 10-year bonds is currently 5.14% compared with 7.75% last July.

The road map is to follow a growth and job creation path. I, for one, hope sincerely that Mr Rajoy and his team can pull it off. How the Spaniards and particularly the young have suffered. And they did not deserve to as my previous rantings on sloppy banking have declared.

The question now is, if Spain can do it (and indeed Ireland), can the UK?

I take your money – you pay me!

Not the godfather speaking but Paul Tucker the deputy sheriff, err sorry mate, deputy Governor of the Bank of England. Threat or blue-sky thinking, you takes your pick.

Those readers who have watched the Danish crime and political dramas in double doses on a UK Saturday night, will appreciate that things Danish are superior. And the Danes have tried Mr Tucker's little trick and made it work.

The underlying problem is this: retail and investment banks (still mixed up by the way) lodge their excess cash with the Bank of England who kindly pay interest on this deposit. But what if that was reversed. Suppose the central bank posted negative interest such that it cost money to hold money with them? The theory goes that this might discourage such lodgements and if so, these banks might do what we all thought all along they were in business to do, that is to say, lend to businesses so they in turn could get on with doing business.

There are a few snags of course. Smaller building societies might go bust since much of their income comes from base-rate tracker mortgages (we will try and forget LIBOR for the present). Secondly, if banks are paying out to the Central Bank instead of gathering in, they can hardly be expected to pay the whopping interest they now pay their depositors, can they? Thus, savers will be bashed again although of course as the Mercedes sales manager said to me recently, "they buy a new car since their money earns nowt in the bank". So, the second negative might be a plus. Just as negative interest might be, you might say.

U.S.A. – Up and away.

Whilst most economic viewers could be forgiven for being distracted by the Near East and the Far East, our cousins in the West have been quietly moving forward.

Whilst little Cyprus has felt the cold wind of the hard winter (why does Germany continue to berate fellow members of the Board when it is itself the MD of the business that has suffered a general failure of management?) and China tries to dampen its growth under a new boss and Japan loosens its financial belt, our friends over the pond have been getting on with things.

One factor easily overlooked is that the US of A is a sort of economic federation. The federal government, that is to say the part we know of in the news, is making substantial cutbacks in spending but left field the US states have been active. Active since by law they are required to balance their budgets. Consequently, and I acknowledge an article by Richard Blackden in New York for this detail, many states have been laying off public employees, lifting taxes and cutting benefits. A good example is California (the largest state by economic power) which has raised income and sales taxes and is on track to generate a first budget surplus in almost ten years.

And, harsh economic needs can shape perceived morality. We recall the harsh treatment handed out to those trying to get on-line gambling a feature of nightlife activity (wire fraud) and I have personal experience of the barriers to gaming machine licence applications. But now, this most modern of ways to get revenue ticking is legal in Delaware, Nevada and soon New Jersey. Massachusetts and Pennsylvania seem likely to follow.

The USA is in growth mode and taken as a whole, the budget deficit may well fall to below $1trillion for the first time since the 2008 crisis began.

The trend in America as witnessed by the continuing strong dollar could well be the reason why world stock markets are optimistic. Europe is important. It is not as important as the USA however.

Come on you Brics.

"The world has a new economic bloc that is the driver of current global growth, and we see that it is under-respresented in the governance structure in the IMF. Maybe this is a challenge the IMF itself has to face over the new few years". This statement by Brazil's trade minister Fernando Pimentel amounts to a call from the collection of nations, Brazil, Russia, India, China and South Africa, for a re-think of the present inclusiveness of the World Bank and the IMF. The Brics believe they are unrepresented and excluded from decisions made about macro funding.

This is not rhetoric. China and Brazil have agreed a currency pact by agreeing to trade up to $30bn a year in their own currencies so as to lessen their dependency on the US dollar and the euro. For Brazil, this amount would represent 40% of its annual trade with China. This deal is intended to guard against future wobbles in international financial markets and avoid any need for outside credit lines.

In addition, the Brics are to create their own development bank to encourage cross-nation trade and give help to any member in a time of crisis.

Taken together, these two new steps are significant since the Brics already make up more than a third of G20 economic output and according to PricewaterhouseCoopers this proportion will reach 50% by 2050.

Come on you Brics: shake the old order up – it is ripe for it.

Eleven months of bull.

Since it was invented in 1984, eleven consecutive months of rising prices is a record for the FTSE 100. And April 013 may well not end the bull charge. Why when all news is war, pestilence and generally bad, is this so?

Investors in equities are realists with money: they know that the "big uns" are stashed with margin, profit and cash whilst all safe havens have gone negative in real terms. Even the orchard across the pond has reportedly got some $100bn of cash beyond its shores and why would Apple bring that back home and pay tax of up to 35% on it? I might be stuck with a 55% withholding tax on my hard-earned pension pot in the UK but the chaps in California can buy back shares and raise the nascent dividend to get rid of their readies.

The fact is that the UK measure is not isolated. The S&P 500 index is up 12% this calendar year so far and houses over there and back home are selling again and at higher prices and built on land bought relatively cheaply (take a look at the 6-month graph of the share price of Taylor Wimpey, the UK's second biggest house builder).

So, we reach May. Do we sell and go away? I do not think so.

Plague on your pennies.

My last article "Eleven months of bull" pronounced that the rise in equity prices had not reached its zenith. This has proved to be so. Just ten days later the FTSE 100 has reached 6,600, its highest point since 2007 and thus before the great crash. It is being pointed out that adding to the factor of stored wealth of the big companies is the increasing unattractiveness of interest rates on deposit money as easing, a la Japan, spreads like a contagion.

The Times quotes George Buckley of Deutsche Bank as pointing out that six central banks have cut their rates this month alone. This means that club UK/USA/Japan has been joined – though not quite at zero – by:-

• ECB

• Central Bank of India

• Poland Central Bank

• Central Bank of Denmark

• Reserve Bank of Australia ....and most recently

• BankofKorea

and these six account for some 23% of global GDP.

If one draws the logical conclusion that these cuts in rates over such a wide spectrum are indicative of monetary stimulus continuing, then it is also logical to assume that global equity rallies in harmony with the UK FTSE 100 will continue.

It is of course a plague on all your pennies depending on which side in the currency war you are on and generally speaking wars of all kinds tend not to produce winners.

Confounding the doomsters.

Official figures from the Office of National Statistics show a UK GDP growth rate in the quarter to June 013 of 0.7% and this is the fastest rate since early 2010. As important, it is being regarded by leading commentators as "balanced" in that the growth was not as had been foreshadowed by the doomsters produced by consumer spending, or rather only 0.2% was. The majority slice of 0.5% GDP growth was down to trade and investment.

Looking more closely at the causes of the UK's economic recovery, manufacturing beat forecasts as did the construction sector. Indeed, the crown jewels of exports and investment represented over half of this second quarter growth rate. In the light of all that has gone on since the dark days since 2008, this really is excellent news. Rob Wood of Berenberg Bank said the UK "was firing on all cylinders" and on track for "a sustainable recovery".

New housing construction is a worthy bellwether of momentum since it is not merely the actual building that is in play but the ancillary feeders of associated products and services. A vital indicative statistic is that of mortgage lending. Figures from the Council of Mortgage Lenders show advances of £16.6bn in July 013 which is a year-on-year growth of 30%. What is particularly significant is that the last single month in which this figure was exceeded was August 2008. The historical significance of this date is highlighted in my book Quantitative Wheezing ISBN 978-1-4466-6609-8 which started recording the credit crisis as from 7th October 2008.

And proof of the pudding is in the building of new homes. Persimmon, the UK's largest builder, reported a 40% jump in first half profits given a recorded 7% increase in house sales. As for the second biggest player, perhaps the siren for the optimism permeating this article is the fact that (for the first time ever for any share) my long-term share holding in Taylor Wimpey is showing a 100% profit.

Just a tiny bubble.

Perspective has always been more relevant than short-term comparatives. This was never more important than when considering all the stuff presently being written about an impending or current "property bubble".

Mortgage approval rates in the UK were around 107,000 a month in the extended period between the millennium year and 2007, that is, the seven years preceding the credit crisis. The average price of a house in 2007 was £186,044: the peak. Whilst it is true that house purchase momentum is rising steeply, this is deceptive in the potential causation of a property bubble. In absolute terms, figures published for the month of July 2013 show mortgage approvals of 60,624 (57% of the figure in the fat years of plenty) with the average buy price of £170,514 according to Nationwide (92% of the same comparator). Plus, price absolutes are deceptive since the big builders are constructing more proper houses and less flats and undoubtedly taking profit advantage of the current lending scheme and the impending help to buy scheme.

So, actually, the bubble is a tiny one and the market does not believe the new B of E's Governor when he forecasts low interest rates for nearly ever-and-a-day. One other factor is that in July 2013, UK consumers put a further £200m on their credit cards so that now a not-so-tiny £57.2bn is outstanding on plastic. A bit of a drag.

Oh no, surely not again.

John Nelson, chairman of Lloyd's of London said recently that the insurance industry (try substituting insurance for banking and 2013 for 2008) needed to be "extremely watchful" and added "Insurance can be a dangerous business for those who do not understand it." Apparently he was talking about "sidecars" but not the ones that do not exist anymore. Rather, about underwriting vehicles that non-insurers can invest in.

According to an article in The Times by Miles Costello, the Prudential Regulation Authority (PRA) is monitoring a cartload of cash coming into the insurance market from hedge funds and pension schemes. Such entry is effected by buying securities that insurance underwriters issue to pass on some of the risks taken on. In a way, so far so good but Guy Carpenter, an insurance broker and consultant, has said that $10 billion has entered the market this month and in total this "alternative" capital now accounts for an estimated $45 billion of insurance risks related to property alone.

Although the PRA does not regulate hedge funds or pension schemes, it is concerned with insurers and the worry is that due to demand, the securities might be sold too cheaply. Such a mispricing of risk resonates with both the fifth anniversary of the bankruptcy of Lehman

Brothers and the righting of Concordia last night off Tuscany. When insurers reinsure, some of the exposure remains in their hands.

Wholesale mortgage market of 2008, sub-prime – sounds familiar? Surely not again.

A market not ours.

An isolated introvert little island we are not. At least as far as the financial market is concerned. New figures from the Office of National Statistics (ONS) show that for the first time, over half of the £1.8 trillion value of the UK stock market is owned by overseas investors. And it is a relatively recent phenomenon. The current 53.2% of non-UK share compares with 43.4% just three years ago and twenty years ago the UK held more than 80% of its value in-house.

The explanation for the growing internationalism of the UK stock market is attributed to global merger and acquisition activity and to a lesser degree the relaxation of ownership rules. What is particularly interesting is that of the whole foreign slice, North America accounts for 48% and Europeans 26%. The next biggest slug is Asian owners with 10%.

Equity holdings by UK pension funds has plunged to an all-time low of 4.7% (the figure was 21.7% in 1998). Henry Tapper of First Actuarial said that tough regulations had forced managers of defined benefit pension schemes to "immunise" the risk of equity volatility "at any cost" and so the movement into safer places such as bonds. Notwithstanding this trend, two other data sets pointed towards more equity investment namely defined contribution pension schemes and the advent of auto-enrolment schemes where equities would feature heavily.

Sounds uncannily like a case of American ponies coming to the rescue again with the Chinese and Indians chasing hard on the rails. Too simplistic of course.

IPOs no longer NONOs.

After five years of near darkness, spotting indicators of a resurgence in UK economic activity is a hard habit to break. So, at least for now, the habit is indulged.

Initial Public Offerings (IPOs) occur when a company is floated on the London stock market and, almost by definition, is a nascent economic trigger. It follows that when in a downer, IPOs dry up and when on a high new finance is sought. EY, the large accountancy firm, has produced figure to show that in the quarter to September 013 £601m was raised and this is an increase of 180% on the equivalent period last year. Furthermore, for the nine months of 2013, IPOs generated more than £3bn, twice that raised in the whole of 2012.

Looking forward, good solid businesses are known to be floating some of their activity including Royal Mail, Stock Spirits Group and Gala Coral.

Then there is the eternal bellwether of new vehicle registrations. According to the Society of Motor Manufacturers, 403,136 sales were made bearing the new 63 plate in September 013 being the highest monthly figure since March 2008 – the year the sky fell in, or rather the tyres were punctured. Performance in Europe is worth hailing too. More than one in seven of all new cars registered in Europe during September was built in the UK with only Germany selling more.

Not all habits are bad. Furthermore, my financial adviser was super-bullish at our annual chat this week. Let the good times roll.

About the author.

John G Smith has had a working life spanning fifty years and divided equally between line management and business advice. He is a qualified accountant and still acts as a strategic adviser.

John Smith is an active trader on the UK and USA stock markets and writes regularly on his website quantitative-wheezing.co.uk about the financial and economic issues of the day.

This website also has some informative set pieces aimed specifically at the business student.

Other books by John G Smith.

Quantitative Wheezing

ISBN 978-1-4466-6609-8

How to wise-up on business & finance

ISBN 978-1-4466-2195-0

Barn door to balance sheet

ISBN 978-1-4461-1930-3

Derbyshire born

ISBN 978-1-4466-7742-1

Poems about